WRIGHT FAMILY RECORDS

PATENT DEEDS AND LAND GRANTS
DEED RECORDS, 1758–1908; LAND TAX LISTS, 1782–1850;
DEATH RECORDS, 1856–1920; PROBATE RECORDS, 1758–1922

BUCKINGHAM COUNTY, VIRGINIA

Robert N. Grant

Heritage Books
2025

HERITAGE BOOKS

AN IMPRINT OF HERITAGE BOOKS, INC.

Books, CDs, and more—Worldwide

For our listing of thousands of titles see our website
at
www.HeritageBooks.com

Published 2025 by
HERITAGE BOOKS, INC.
Publishing Division
5810 Ruatan Street
Berwyn Heights, MD 20740

International Standard Book Number
Paperbound: 978-0-7884-5117-1

WRIGHT FAMILY RECORDS

PATENT DEEDS AND LAND GRANTS

BUCKINGHAM COUNTY, VIRGINIA

Revised as of June 30, 2025

This document is an appendix to a larger work titled *Sorting Some Of The Wrights Of Southern Virginia*. The work is divided into parts for each family of Wrights that has been researched. Each part is divided into two sections; the first section is text discussing the family and the evidence supporting the relationships and the second section is a descendants chart summarizing the relationships and information known about each individual.

The appendices to the work (of which this document is one) present source records for persons named Wright by county and by type of record with the identification of the person named and their Wright ancestors to the extent known.

The sources for the records listed in this appendix are the following:

1) Virginia, Index to Patents 1623-1774, Alphabetically and by Book, microfilm #29308, Genealogical Society of the Church of Jesus Christ of the Latter Day Saints and Patent Deeds available from The Virginia State Library, Richmond, Virginia 23219.

The identification of a person or their ancestor by year and county indicates their year of death and county of residence at death. For example, "1763 Thomas Wright of Bedford County" indicates that this was the Thomas Wright who died in 1763 in Bedford County. If no state is listed after the county, the state is Virginia; counties in states other than Virginia will have a state listed after the county, as in "1876 William S. Wright of Highland County, Ohio".

A parenthetical after the name indicates an identification of the person when a place of death is not yet known, as in "John Wright (Goochland County Carpenter)". A county in parentheses after the name indicates the county with which that person was most identified when no evidence of the place of death has yet been found, as in "Grief Wright (Bedford County)".

All or portions of the text and descendants charts for each Wright family identified are available from the author:

Robert N. Grant
15 Campo Bello Court   (H) 650-854-0895
Menlo Park, California 94025   RNGrant@grantandgordon.com

This is a work in process and I would be most interested in receiving additional information about any of the persons identified in these records in order to correct any errors or expand on the information given.

Appendix: Buckingham County, Virginia, Land Grants

Book/Page	Date	Name	Description	Identification
P.D. 35/220	1763/07/07	John Wright	272 acres on north side of Appomattox River	Probably 1826 John Wright of Buckingham County
L.G. F/505	1782/06/01	John Wright	322 acres on Bent Creek	1826 John Wright of Buckingham County
L.G. 56/481	1808/11/08	John Wright	40 acres	1826 John Wright of Buckingham County

WRIGHT FAMILY

DEED RECORDS

1758 TO 1908

BUCKINGHAM COUNTY, VIRGINIA

Revised as of June 30, 2025

Introduction To Appendix: Deed Records for Buckingham County, Virginia

This document is an appendix to a larger work titled *Sorting Some Of The Wrights Of Southern Virginia*. The work is divided into parts for each family of Wrights that has been researched. Each part is divided into two sections; the first section is text discussing the family and the evidence supporting the relationships and the second section is a descendants chart summarizing the relationships and information known about each individual.

The appendices to the work (of which this document is one) present source records for persons named Wright by county and by type of record with the identification of the person named and their Wright ancestors to the extent known.

The sources for the records listed in this appendix are the following:

1) Buckingham County, Virginia, Deed Records, available from the Clerk of the Circuit Court, P.O. Box 107, Buckingham, Virginia 23921.

2) Genealogical Records of Buckingham County, Virginia, by Edythe Rucker Whitely, Genealogical Publishing Co., Inc., 1984.

3) Buckingham County, Virginia, Records, Land Tax Summaries & Implied Deeds, Volume 1 1782-1814 & Volume 2 1815-1840, by Roger G. Ward, Iberian Publishing Company, Athens, Georgia, 548 Cedar Creek Drive, Athens, Georgia 30605, 1994.

The identification of a person or their ancestor by year and county indicates their year of death and county of residence at death. For example, "1763 Thomas Wright of Bedford County" indicates that this was the Thomas Wright who died in 1763 in Bedford County. If no state is listed after the county, the state is Virginia; counties in states other than Virginia will have a state listed after the county, as in "1876 William S. Wright of Highland County, Ohio".

A parenthetical after the name indicates an identification of the person when a place of death is not yet known, as in "John Wright (Goochland County Carpenter)". A county in parentheses after the name indicates the county with which that person was most identified when no evidence of the place of death has yet been found, as in "Grief Wright (Bedford County)".

All or portions of the text and descendants charts for each Wright family identified are available from the author:

Robert N. Grant
15 Campo Bello Court   (H) 650-854-0895
Menlo Park, California 94025   RNGrant@grantandgordon.com

This is a work in progress and I would be most interested in receiving additional information about any of the persons identified in these records in order to correct any errors or expand on the information given.

Appendix: Buckingham County, Virginia, Deed Records:

Book/Page		Date	Grantor	Grantee	Instrument	Identification
04	303	1843/02/28	William W. Ferguson & Sarah A. M. Ferguson	Andrew Wright, Trustee for Thomas Wright and others	D. T.	
01	192	1864/03/15	Edmund W. Cabell & Elizabeth T. Cabell	James A. Wright, Trustee	D. T.	1891 James A. Wright of Buckingham County, son of 1842 Thomas Wright of Buckingham County, grandson of 1813 John Wright of Buckingham County, and great grandson of 1809 John Wright of Buckingham County
01	453	1867/07/15	James A. Wright	Geo. D. Saunders, Tr.	D. T.	1891 James A. Wright of Buckingham County, son of 1842 Thomas Wright of Buckingham County, grandson of 1813 John Wright of Buckingham County, and great grandson of 1809 John Wright of Buckingham County
02	274	1869/03/08	James A. Wright	Charles R. Shepherd, Tr.	D. T.	1891 James A. Wright of Buckingham County, son of 1842 Thomas Wright of Buckingham County, grandson of 1813 John Wright of Buckingham County, and great grandson of 1809 John Wright of Buckingham County
01	123	1869/04/29	Wm. R. Wright	Nannie D. Wright & Virginia P. Wright	Gift Deed	1871 William R. Wright of Buckingham County, son of 1842 Thomas Wright of Buckingham County, grandson of 1813 John Wright of Buckingham County, and great grandson of 1809 John Wright of Buckingham County
01	124	1869/04/29	Wm. R. Wright	Thos. Wright & Wm. H. Wright	Gift Deed	1871 William R. Wright of Buckingham County, son of 1842 Thomas Wright of Buckingham County, grandson of 1813 John Wright of Buckingham County, and great grandson of 1809 John Wright of Buckingham County
01	488	1870/04/26	Jas. A. Wright, as Sheriff and administrator of Benjamin Whitehead	Jos. William Hebditch	B. & S.	1891 James A. Wright of Buckingham County, son of 1842 Thomas Wright of Buckingham County, grandson of 1813 John Wright of Buckingham County, and great grandson of 1809 John Wright of Buckingham County

Appendix: Buckingham County, Virginia, Deed Records:

Book/Page		Date	Grantor	Grantee	Instrument	Identification
01	201	1870/04/19	Jas. A. Wright, as Sheriff and administrator of Richard Moseley	John C. Turner	Lis Pendens	1891 James A. Wright of Buckingham County, son of 1842 Thomas Wright of Buckingham County, grandson of 1813 John Wright of Buckingham County, and great grandson of 1809 John Wright of Buckingham County
02	470	1872/04/22	Richard Malone & Mary Ann Malone	Pattie L. Wright	Gift	
01	571	1872/03/18	James A. Wright, as executor of William B. Jones, and others	Exors of Thos. M. Bondurant	Lis Pendens	1891 James A. Wright of Buckingham County, son of 1842 Thomas Wright of Buckingham County, grandson of 1813 John Wright of Buckingham County, and great grandson of 1809 John Wright of Buckingham County
02	106	1873/05/31	Hugh R. Patteson	L. H. Wright	B. & S.	Leonard H. Wright, son of Charles Wright and grandson of Robert Wright, Sr. (Campbell County)
02	729	1874/01/05	Wm. Perkins, Sp'l Comr.	James A. Wright (by Comr)	Deed	1891 James A. Wright of Buckingham County, son of 1842 Thomas Wright of Buckingham County, grandson of 1813 John Wright of Buckingham County, and great grandson of 1809 John Wright of Buckingham County
02	469	1874/01/23	Richard Malone & Mary Ann Malone	Margaret Wright	Gift Deed	
02	350	1875/03/10	Joel T. Moorman, Exor.	Thomas Wright, administrator of William R. Wright & Thomas Wright & William H. Wright & Edmund W. Cabell & Elizabeth Cabell & C. W. Dickens & Virginia P. Dickens & Levina Wright	Lis Pendens	Heirs of 1871 William R. Wright of Buckingham County, son of 1842 Thomas Wright of Buckingham County, grandson of 1813 John Wright of Buckingham County, and great grandson of 1809 John Wright of Buckingham County

Appendix: Buckingham County, Virginia, Deed Records:

Book/Page		Date	Grantor	Grantee	Instrument	Identification
02	351	1875/03/10	Joel T. Moorman, Exor.	Thomas Wright, administrator of William R. Wright & Thomas Wright & William H. Wright & Levina Wright	Lis Pendens	Heirs of 1871 William R. Wright of Buckingham County, son of 1842 Thomas Wright of Buckingham County, grandson of 1813 John Wright of Buckingham County, and great grandson of 1809 John Wright of Buckingham County
02	523	1876/06/29	L. H. Wright & Bettie L. Wright	Henry Douglass	B. & S.	Leonard H. Wright, son of Charles Wright and grandson of Robert Wright, Sr. (Campbell County)
02	518	1876/07/10	James A. Wright, Comr.	William M. Cabell	B. & S.	1892 James A. Wright of Buckingham County, son of 1842 Thomas Wright of Buckingham County, grandson of 1813 John Wright of Buckingham County, and great grandson of 1809 John Wright of Buckingham County
02	469	1874/01/23	Richard Malone & Mary Ann Malone	Margaret Wright	B. & S.	
03	076	1877/06/11	Jas. A. Wright & Fannie A. Wright	G. B. Hanes, Tr.	D. T.	1891 James A. Wright of Buckingham County, son of 1842 Thomas Wright of Buckingham County, grandson of 1813 John Wright of Buckingham County, and great grandson of 1809 John Wright of Buckingham County
02	600	1877/01/05	James A. Wright	Wm. J. Spencer	Contract	1891 James A. Wright of Buckingham County, son of 1842 Thomas Wright of Buckingham County, grandson of 1813 John Wright of Buckingham County, and great grandson of 1809 John Wright of Buckingham County
02	663	1877/03/15	Sallie H. Moseley	Bettie L. Wright	B. & S.	Bettie Lee (Patterson) Wright, wife of Leonard H. Wright, a son of Charles Wright and grandson of Robert Wright, Sr. (Campbell County)
02	624	1877/05/07	Samuel Amos	Thomas J. Wright	B. & S.	Thomas J. Wright, son of 1871 William Wright of Buckingham County, grandson of 1842 Thomas Wright of Buckingham County, great grandson of 1813 John Wright of Buckingham County, and great great grandson of 1809 John Wright of Buckingham County

Appendix: Buckingham County, Virginia, Deed Records:

Book/Page		Date	Grantor	Grantee	Instrument	Identification
03	108	1878/10/19	James A. Wright	P. A. Forbes	B. & S.	1891 James A. Wright of Buckingham County, son of 1842 Thomas Wright of Buckingham County, grandson of 1813 John Wright of Buckingham County, and great grandson of 1809 John Wright of Buckingham County
03	151	1878/05/13	James A. Wright & Langdon C. Moseley, Sheriff	Wm. M. Cabell	B. & S.	1891 James A. Wright of Buckingham County, son of 1842 Thomas Wright of Buckingham County, grandson of 1813 John Wright of Buckingham County, and great grandson of 1809 John Wright of Buckingham County
03	105	1878/05/18	Sallie H. Moseley	Bettie L. Wright	B. & S.	Bettie Lee (Patterson) Wright, wife of Leonard H. Wright, a son of Charles Wright and grandson of Robert Wright, Sr. (Campbell County)
03	129	1879/01/14	James A. Wright (sub Tr.)	Celia B. Payne & Susan L. Payne	B. & S.	1891 James A. Wright of Buckingham County, son of 1842 Thomas Wright of Buckingham County, grandson of 1813 John Wright of Buckingham County, and great grandson of 1809 John Wright of Buckingham County
03	259	1879/10/14	Thomas P. Wright	Thomas M. Wright	B. & S.	Grantor: 1880 Thomas P. Wright of Buckingham County, son of 1840 David M. Wright, Sr. (Buckingham County) Grantee: Thomas Monroe Wright, son of 1880 Thomas P. Wright of Buckingham County and grandson of 1840 David M. Wright, Sr. (Buckingham County)
03	507	1880/09/14	Jas. A. Wright & Fannie A. Wright	Willis Wright & Geo. W. Bennett & Granderson Watson, Trustees of St. Jory Baptist Church	Gift Deed	Grantor: 1891 James A. Wright of Buckingham County, son of 1842 Thomas Wright of Buckingham County Grantee: Willis Wright, son of 1892 Dick Wright of Buckingham County
03	421	1880/07/09	James A. Wright, Jr.	Richmond & Southwestern R.R. Co.	Deed	

Appendix: Buckingham County, Virginia, Deed Records:

Book/Page		Date	Grantor	Grantee	Instrument	Identification
03	544	1880/05/26	Margaret Wright & J. L. Wright & Pattie L. Wright	Robert H. Gilliam	B. & H.	
03	391	1880/04/27	P. A. Forbes & Helen M. Forbes	Iverson Wright	B. & S.	1926 Iverson Twyman Wright of Shelby County, Tennessee, son of 1891 James A. Wright of Buckingham County, grandson of 1842 Thomas Wright of Buckingham County, great grandson of 1813 John Wright of Buckingham County, and great great grandson of 1809 John Wright of Buckingham County
03	373	1880/04/23	William A. Moss & Patty A. Moss	James A. Wright, Jr.	B. & S.	James A. Wright, Jr., son of 1891 James A. Wright of Buckingham County, grandson of 1842 Thomas Wright of Buckingham County, great grandson of 1813 John Wright of Buckingham County, and great great grandson of 1809 John Wright of Buckingham County
03	530	1880/12/07	William A. Moss & Patty A. Moss	James A. Wright, Jr., Tr.	D. T.	James A. Wright, Jr., son of 1891 James A. Wright of Buckingham County, grandson of 1842 Thomas Wright of Buckingham County, great grandson of 1813 John Wright of Buckingham County, and great great grandson of 1809 John Wright of Buckingham County
03	532	1880/12/07	William A. Moss & Patty A. Moss	James A. Wright, Jr., Tr.	D. T.	James A. Wright, Jr., son of 1891 James A. Wright of Buckingham County, grandson of 1842 Thomas Wright of Buckingham County, great grandson of 1813 John Wright of Buckingham County, and great great grandson of 1809 John Wright of Buckingham County
03	534	1880/12/08	William A. Moss & Pattie A. Moss	James A. Wright, Jr.	B. & S.	James A. Wright, Jr., son of 1891 James A. Wright of Buckingham County, grandson of 1842 Thomas Wright of Buckingham County, great grandson of 1813 John Wright of Buckingham County, and great great grandson of 1809 John Wright of Buckingham County
04	067	1881/06/17	Jas. A. Wright	J. B. Gilliam, Tr.	D. T.	

Appendix: Buckingham County, Virginia, Deed Records:

Book/Page		Date	Grantor	Grantee	Instrument	Identification
04	092	1881/07/20	James A. Wright, Jr.	Lackey A. McCraw	B. & S.	James A. Wright, Jr., son of 1891 James A. Wright of Buckingham County, grandson of 1842 Thomas Wright of Buckingham County, great grandson of 1813 John Wright of Buckingham County, and great great grandson of 1809 John Wright of Buckingham County
04	092	1881/08/08	Jas. A. Wright, Jr. & Iverson Wright	James S. Allen	B. & S.	James A. Wright, Jr., and 1926 Iverson Wright of Shelby County, Tennessee, sons of 1891 James A. Wright of Buckingham County, grandsons of 1842 Thomas Wright of Buckingham County, great grandsons of 1813 John Wright of Buckingham County, and great great grandsons of 1809 John Wright of Buckingham County
04	047	1881/04/22	James A. Wright, Jr., Tr. &c.	Rob't A. Baldwin	B. & S.	James A. Wright, Jr., son of 1891 James A. Wright of Buckingham County, grandson of 1842 Thomas Wright of Buckingham County, great grandson of 1813 John Wright of Buckingham County, and great great grandson of 1809 John Wright of Buckingham County
04	101	1881/03/30	James L. Wright & J. F. Edwards &	Ann E. Edwards & Margaret Wright & Virginia L. Chiles & C. J. Chiles & Pattie L. Wright	Par.	
04	091	1881/08/04	Iverson Wright	J. A. Wright, Trustee	D. T.	1926 Iverson Twyman Wright of Shelby County, Tennessee, son of 1891 James A. Wright of Buckingham County, grandson of 1842 Thomas Wright of Buckingham County, great grandson of 1813 John Wright of Buckingham County, and great great grandson of 1809 John Wright of Buckingham County
04	337	1882/11/20	J. W. Harris & Mollie J. Harris	L. H. Wright	B. & S.	Leonard H. Wright, son of Charles Wright and grandson of Robert Wright, Sr., (Campbell County)
04	338	1882/11/28	L. H. Wright & Bettie L. Wright	Henry Taylor	B. & S.	Leonard H. Wright, son of Charles Wright and grandson of Robert Wright, Sr. (Campbell County)

Appendix: Buckingham County, Virginia, Deed Records:

Book/Page		Date	Grantor	Grantee	Instrument	Identification
04	339	1882/11/28	Henry Taylor & Eliza Taylor	J. B. Gillian, Trustee	D. T.	
04	506	1883/09/20	Jas. A. Wright & R. M. Dickinson, Commissioner	R. M. Anderson, Trustee	D. T.	
04	548	1884/01/26	James A. Wright, as executor of William B. Jones & Thomas W. Garrett & Ann Elizabeth (Wright) Garrett	Joel T. Moorman, Exor of Elizabeth Jones	Lis Pendens	

Appendix: Buckingham County, Virginia, Deed Records:

Book/Page		Date	Grantor	Grantee	Instrument	Identification
04	562	1884/02/15	Thomas J. Wright, administrator of William R. Wright & Thomas J. Wright & Lavinia Wright & Edmund W. Cabell & Elizabeth (Cabell) Wright & Charles W. Dickens & Virginia P. (Wright) Dickens & L. C. Moseley, administrator of William H. Wright & Vic Wright & Witey Wright & Dallas Wright & Clifford Wright & Alice Wright & Lockey Wright & Anna D. (Wright) Meginnson, deceased & James A. Wright, as executor of William B. Jones	Joel T. Moorman, Exor of Elizabeth Jones	Lis Pendens	Estate of 1871 William R. Wright of Buckingham County, son of 1842 Thomas Wright of Buckingham County, grandson of 1813 John Wright of Buckingham County, and great grandson of 1809 John Wright of Buckingham County
05	018	1884/06/21	Jessie F. Toney	Bettie B. Wright	Gift	Bettie B. (Toney) Wright, wife of Charles E. Wright, a son of 1863 William Wright of Buckingham County, probably grandson of 1803 John Wright of Cumberland County, great grandson of 1770 John Wright of Cumberland County, and great great grandson of 1769 George Wright of Essex County
05	019	1884/00/00	Alex. J. Bondurant & Emily M. Bondurant	Reuben Wright	B. & S.	

Appendix: Buckingham County, Virginia, Deed Records:

Book/Page		Date	Grantor	Grantee	Instrument	Identification
04	527	1883/11/08	William M. Cabell & Mildred K. Cabell	Thomas I. Wright J. T. Moorman & William A. Moore & John P. Hackett & Thomas H. Roberts & Thomas J. Wright & Samuel F. Abraham & David Sudsberry	Gift	
05	262	1885/07/20	A. T. Moseley, Trustee for Maria L. Moseley	Thomas J. Wright & C. W. Hardiman	B. & S.	
05	445	1886/04/15	James L. Wright & Pattie L. Wright	James F. Edwards	B. & S.	
06	020	1886/05/31	Margaret Wright & S. A. Spencer & Mary S. Spencer & J. M. Edwards & Bessie J. Edwards & C. J. Chiles & Virginia L. Chiles	Charles H. Anderson	B. & S.	
06	007	1886/04/20	Estate of Thomas F. Wright	Thos. U. Wright & Joseph T. Spencer & Polly Spencer & William J. Wright & Thomas J. Robertson & Nannie Robertson & Tiberius W. Robertson & Anderson T. Wright	Partition	Estate of 1873 Thomas F. Wright of Buckingham County, probably a son of 1842 Thomas Wright of Buckingham County, grandson of 1813 John Wright of Buckingham County, and great grandson of 1809 John Wright of Buckingham County

Appendix: Buckingham County, Virginia, Deed Records:

Book/Page		Date	Grantor	Grantee	Instrument	Identification
05	404	1886/04/17	Jessie F. Toney & Eliza Toney	Bettie B. Wright	Gift	Bettie B. (Toney) Wright, wife of Charles E. Wright, a son of 1863 William Wright of Buckingham County, grandson of 1803 John Wright of Cumberland County, great grandson of 1770 John Wright of Cumberland County, and great great grandson of 1769 George Wright of Essex County
05	360	1886/03/08	John B. Gilliam, Trustee	James A. Wright, Jr.	B. & S.	
06	142	1888/01/14	Bettie L. Wright		Homestead	Bettie Lee (Patterson) Wright, wife of Leonard H. Wright, a son of Charles Wright and grandson of Robert Wright, Sr. (Campbell County)
06	427	1888/03/30	Bettie L. Wright & Lucy J. Patterson & William S. Patterson	Royal N. Williams & Nathaniel Walter Williams	B. & S.	Bettie Lee (Patterson) Wright, wife of Leonard H. Wright, a son of Charles Wright and grandson of Robert Wright, Sr. (Campbell County)
06	227	1888/05/02	Thos. M. Leitch's Est.	Josie L. Wright & al.	Par. by decree	
07	051	1889/12/13	Joseph T. Spencer & Mary S. Spencer	Thomas U. Wright's Estate	B. & S.	Thomas V. or U. Wright, son of 1873 Thomas F. Wright of Buckingham County, probably grandson of 1842 Thomas Wright of Buckingham County, great grandson of 1813 John Wright of Buckingham County, and great great grandson of 1809 John Wright of Buckingham County
06	438	1889/06/00	Geo. Van Dine & F. E. Van Dine	Wm. Wright	B. & S.	
06	514	1890/01/27	James A. Wright & Frances A. Wright	O. T. Wicker & J. M. Crute & C. C. Fleming, Trustees of Farmville Bldg. & Trust Co.	D. T.	1891 James A. Wright of Buckingham County, son of 1842 Thomas Wright of Buckingham County, grandson of 1813 John Wright of Buckingham County, and great grandson of 1809 John Wright of Buckingham County
07	305	1891/05/08	J. A. Wright & J. T. Wright	Paulett, Son & Co.	Crop. Lien	

Appendix: Buckingham County, Virginia, Deed Records:

Book/Page		Date	Grantor	Grantee	Instrument	Identification
07	492	1892/05/10	William M. Cabell & Mildred K. Cabell	Roland Wright	B. & S.	Roland P. Wright, son of 1880 Thomas P. Wright of Buckingham County and grandson of 1840 David M. Wright, Sr. (Buckingham County)
07	505	1892/06/27	Frances A. Wright's Admr. C. T. A. & Jas. A. Wright's Exor.	Martha E. Twyman & al.	Lis Pendens	Estate of 1891 James Wright of Buckingham County, son of 1842 Thomas Wright of Buckingham County, grandson of 1813 John Wright of Buckingham County, and great grandson of 1809 John Wright of Buckingham County
07	386	1892/01/21	Pattie L. Wright & W. H. Spencer & Ruth A. Spencer	Charles H. Anderson	B. & S.	
07	495	1891/09/02	Wm. J. Wright & Addie Sue Wright & John A. McFadden	David C. Robertson	D. B. & S.	William J. Wright, son of 1873 Thomas F. Wright of Buckingham County, probably grandson of 1842 Thomas Wright of Buckingham County, great grandson of 1813 John Wright of Buckingham County, and great great grandson of 1809 John Wright of Buckingham County
09	069	1893/08/07	James F. Edwards	W. R. Wright	B. & S.	
09	070	1893/08/17	James M Edwards & Mary F. Edwards	W. R. Wright	B. & S.	
09	070	1896/03/02	James M. Edwards & Mary F. Edwards	W. R. Wright	B. & S.	
08	198	1894/02/09	Thomas J. Wright & Bettie H. Wright	Jerry McFadden	B. & S.	Thomas J. Wright, son of 1871 William Wright of Buckingham County, grandson of 1842 Thomas Wright of Buckingham County, great grandson of 1813 John Wright of Buckingham County, and great great grandson of 1809 John Wright of Buckingham County
08	233	1894/04/16	Charles H. Pendleton & Lucy J. Pendleton	Archer Wright	B. & S.	

Appendix: Buckingham County, Virginia, Deed Records:

Book/Page		Date	Grantor	Grantee	Instrument	Identification
08	562	1895/08/15	Josie L. Wright & William Leitch & Mary Leitch & Mary L. Segar & Jno. C. Segar & Annie L. Lancaster & Nat Lancaster	O. L. Anderson	B. & S.	
09	366	1898/01/10	James A. Wright (by Com)	Richard H. Payne	B. & S.	
10	022	1896/09/30	William R. Wright & Lillie V. Wright & Nannie V. Wright & Mrs. S. A. McGehee & George E. McGehee & Charles H. Anderson & Ella S. Anderson	James H. Bradley	B. & S.	
09	406	1897/12/04	Augustus Wright & Mary C. Wright	George H. Reed	B. & S.	
09	299	1897/01/06	J. T. Wright & M. M. Wright	C. T. McCraw	B. & S.	
09	405	1897/10/28	J. P. Fitzgerald, Sp'l - Comr	Augustus Wright	B. & S.	
09	402	1898/02/26	Archer Wright	Phillip S. Moss	B. & S.	
09	394	1898/02/14	James A. Wright (by Comr.)	E. C. Cook &c.	B. & S.	

Appendix: Buckingham County, Virginia, Deed Records:

Book/Page		Date	Grantor	Grantee	Instrument	Identification
09	517	1888/09/10	L. A. Miller	Bettie H. Wright	Gift	Bettie H. (Miller) Wright, wife of Thomas J. Wright, a son of 1871 William R. Wright of Buckingham County, grandson of 1842 Thomas Wright of Buckingham County, great grandson of 1813 John Wright of Buckingham County, and great great grandson of 1809 John Wright of Buckingham County
09	591	1898/11/30	Geo. C. Walton & Marie A. Walton	Thomas J. Wright	B. & S.	Thomas J. Wright, son of 1871 William Wright of Buckingham County, grandson of 1842 Thomas Wright of Buckingham County, great grandson of 1813 John Wright of Buckingham County, and great great grandson of 1809 John Wright of Buckingham County
09	577	1898/12/19	A. Gordon Moss & Richetta Moss	W. R. Wright	B. & S.	
10	226	1899/11/18	Thomas J. Wright & Bettie H. Wright	James W. Wright	Gift	Grantor: Thomas J. Wright, son of 1871 William Wright of Buckingham County, grandson of 1842 Thomas Wright of Buckingham County, great grandson of 1813 John Wright of Buckingham County, and great great grandson of 1809 John Wright of Buckingham County Grantee: James W. Wright, son of Thomas J. Wright, grandson of 1871 William Wright of Buckingham County, great grandson of 1842 Thomas Wright of Buckingham County, great great grandson of 1813 John Wright of Buckingham County, and great great great grandson of 1809 John Wright of Buckingham County
11	022	1900/12/18	Nannie V. Wright & W. R. Wright & Lillie V. Wright & A. S. McGehee & Geo. E. McGehee	Charles H. Anderson	B. & S.	
10	481	1900/08/29	Wm. R. Wright's Estate	W. E. Swann	Tax Deed	
10	512	1900/10/24	Wm. R. Wright's Estate	W. E. Swann	Tax Deed	

Appendix: Buckingham County, Virginia, Deed Records:

Book/Page		Date	Grantor	Grantee	Instrument	Identification
10	536	1900/09/28	George H. Reed & Margaret Ann Reed	Augustus Wright	B. & S.	
10	261	1900/01/17	Mildred K. Cabell	Trent Wright	B. & S.	Trent Wright, son of 1892 Dick Wright of Buckingham County
11	166	1901/12/13	Aug. Wright (Pres. S. Ry H Co)	Merchants Trust Co. sub. tr.	Resolution	
11	316	1895/01/29	William Bryant & Mary Susan Wright	Bob Wright	B. & S.	
11	358	1902/05/20	Augustus Wright & Mary C. Wright	Russel Martin	B. & S.	
11	450	1902/10/16	W. R. Wright & Lillie V. Wright & Charles H. Anderson & Ella S. Anderson & Geo E. McGehee & Allie S. McGehee & Edward G. Winston & Nannie V. Winston	W. J. Harvey	B. & S.	
12	053	1903/06/22	Thomas J. Wright & Bettie H. Wright	Nannie P. Goodin & Eva L. Cabell & Sarah M. Lythgoe	Gift	Thomas J. Wright, son of 1871 William Wright of Buckingham County, grandson of 1842 Thomas Wright of Buckingham County, great grandson of 1813 John Wright of Buckingham County, and great great grandson of 1809 John Wright of Buckingham County
12	054	1903/06/22	Thomas J. Wright & Bettie H. Wright	Thomas Jackson Wright	Gift	Thomas J. Wright, son of 1871 William Wright of Buckingham County, grandson of 1842 Thomas Wright of Buckingham County, great grandson of 1813 John Wright of Buckingham County, and great great grandson of 1809 John Wright of Buckingham County
12	174	1904/05/09	R. M. Anderson & Mary B. Anderson	Willis Wright	B. & S.	Willis Wright, son of 1892 Dick Wright of Buckingham County

Appendix: Buckingham County, Virginia, Deed Records:

Book/Page		Date	Grantor	Grantee	Instrument	Identification
12	175	1904/05/09	Willis Wright & Cornelia Edna Wright	A. S. Gilliam, Trustee	D. T.	Willis Wright, son of 1892 Dick Wright of Buckingham County
12	257	1904/09/05	Camm Patteson & H. D. Flood, Special Comrs.	Charles Wright	B. & S.	
13	465	1905/06/29	R. T. Miller & E. B. Miller & G. D. Miller & Minnie M. Given	James W. Wright	B. & S.	
13	254	1906/09/06	A. W. Moore & Watsey E. Moore	Charles E. Wright	B. & S.	
13	464	1906/06/26	T. J. S. Robertson & R. L. Vest & M. E. Vest	James W. Wright	B. & S.	
13	509	1907/00/00	Susie B. Clark & James A. Clark	Charles E. Wright	B. & S.	
15	130	1908/06/29	Charles Wright & Estelle Wright	Maria Davis & Robert Davis & Winston Davis & Nannie Davis	Partition	
15	127	1908/06/09	A. S. Hall, Comr.	Charles Wright & Maria Davis & Winston Davis	B. & S.	

WRIGHT FAMILY

LAND TAX LISTS

1782 TO 1850

BUCKINGHAM COUNTY, VIRGINIA

Revised as of June 30, 2025

Introduction To Appendix: Land Tax Records, Buckingham County, Virginia

This document is an appendix to a larger work titled *Sorting Some Of The Wrights Of Southern Virginia*. The work is divided into parts for each family of Wrights that has been researched. Each part is divided into two sections; the first section is text discussing the family and the evidence supporting the relationships and the second section is a descendants chart summarizing the relationships and information known about each individual.

The appendices to the work (of which this document is one) present source records for persons named Wright by county and by type of record with the identification of the person named and their Wright ancestors to the extent known.

The source for the records listed in this appendix is the following:

1)   Buckingham County, Virginia, Land Tax Lists, available from the Virginia State Archives, 11th & Capitol Streets, Richmond, Virginia 23219, and from FamilySearch.org at http://www.familysearch.org.

The identification of a person or their ancestor by year and county indicates their year of death and county of residence at death. For example, "1763 Thomas Wright of Bedford County" indicates that this was the Thomas Wright who died in 1763 in Bedford County. If no state is listed after the county, the state is Virginia; counties in states other than Virginia will have a state listed after the county, as in "1876 William S. Wright of Highland County, Ohio".

A parenthetical after the name indicates an identification of the person when a place of death is not yet known, as in "John Wright (Goochland County Carpenter)". A county in parentheses after the name indicates the county with which that person was most identified when no evidence of the place of death has yet been found, as in "Grief Wright (Bedford County)".

All or portions of the text and descendants charts for each Wright family identified are available from the author:

Robert N. Grant
15 Campo Bello Court   (H) 650-854-0895
Menlo Park, California 94025   RNGrant@grantandgordon.com

This is a work in process and I would be most interested in receiving additional information about any of the persons identified in these records in order to correct any errors or expand on the information given.

1653(063025)

1782 LAND TAX LIST

BUCKINGHAM COUNTY, VIRGINIA

Appendix: Buckingham County, Virginia, 1782 Land Tax List:

John Bernard and John Moseley Assessment:

Persons names	Quantity	Price	Tax	Identification
Archiblad Wright (Cumbd.)	220	3/2 40	0.8.0	1810 Archibald Wright of Buckingham County, son of 1774 George Wright of Cumberland County and grandson of 1769 George Wright of Essex County
John Wright Senr.	150	2/ 15	0.3.0	1809 John Wright of Buckingham County
John Wright (Potter)	285	2/10 40	0.2.0	1826 John Wright of Buckingham County
Thomas Wright (Amherst)	400	2/ 40	0.8.0	

1783 LAND TAX LIST

BUCKINGHAM COUNTY, VIRGINIA

Appendix: Buckingham County, Virginia, 1783 Land Tax List:

<u>Alterations:</u>

<u>Present Proprietors Names</u>	Qty of <u>Land</u>	Value <u>p Acre</u>	<u>Amount</u>	1½ p <u>Cent</u>	<u>Identification</u>
James Duncan from Wright Richard Execr	200	9/4	93.60	1.0.0	

1784 LAND TAX LIST

BUCKINGHAM COUNTY, VIRGINIA

Appendix: Buckingham County, Virginia, 1784 Land Tax List:

Alterations:

Present Proprietors Names	Qty of Land	Value p Acre	Amount	1½ p Cent	Identification

No Wrights listed

1785 LAND TAX LIST

BUCKINGHAM COUNTY, VIRGINIA

Appendix: Buckingham County, Virginia, 1785 Land Tax List:

<u>Alterations</u>:

<u>Present Proprietors Names</u>	Qty of <u>Land</u>	Value <u>p Acre</u>	<u>Amount</u>	1½ p <u>Cent</u>	<u>Identification</u>
No Wrights listed					

1786 LAND TAX LIST

BUCKINGHAM COUNTY, VIRGINIA

Appendix: Buckingham County, Virginia, 1786 Land Tax List:

<u>Alterations</u>:

<u>Present Proprietors Names</u>	Qty of <u>Land</u>	Value <u>p Acre</u>	<u>Amount</u>	1½ p <u>Cent</u>	<u>Identification</u>

No Wrights listed

1787 LAND TAX LIST

BUCKINGHAM COUNTY, VIRGINIA

Appendix: Buckingham County, Virginia, 1787 Land Tax List

Proprietors Names	Quantity of Land	Value p acre	Amount	1½ p lot	Identification
Archibald (Cumbd)	220	4/4	47.13.4	0.14.1½	1810 Archibald Wright of Buckingham County, son of 1774 George Wright of Cumberland County and grandson of 1769 George Wright of Essex County
John Wright Senr	150	2/4	17.10.0	0.5.3	1809 John Wright of Buckingham County
John Wright (Potter)	285	3/4	47.10.0	0.14.2	1826 John Wright of Buckingham County
John Wright Jur.	322	2/	32.4.0	0.9.7	John Wright, Jr., son of 1826 John Wright of Buckingham County
Thomas Wright (Amherst)	400	2/4	46.13.4	0.14.0	

1788 LAND TAX LIST

BUCKINGHAM COUNTY, VIRGINIA

Appendix: Buckingham County, Virginia, 1788 Land Tax List:

Peter Guerrant District:

Proprietors Names	Quty of Land	Value p Acre	Amount	1½ p. Cent	Identification
Archibald Wright	220	4/4	47.13.4	0.14.1½	1810 Archibald Wright of Buckingham County, son of 1774 George Wright of Cumberland County and grandson of 1769 George Wright of Essex County

Appendix: Buckingham County, Virginia, 1788 Land Tax List:

Josias Jones District:

Proprietors Names	Quantity of Land	Value p Acre	Amount	1½ p Cent	Identification
John Wright Sr	150	2/4	17.10.0	0.5.3	1809 John Wright of Buckingham County
John Wright (Potter)	285	3/4	47.10.0	0.1½.2	1826 John Wright of Buckingham County
John Wright Jr	322	2/	32.4.0	0.9.7	John Wright, Jr., son of 1826 John Wright of Buckingham County
Thomas Wright (Amht)	400	2/4	46.13.4	0.1½.0	

1789 LAND TAX LIST

BUCKINGHAM COUNTY, VIRGINIA

Appendix: Buckingham County, Virginia, 1789 Land Tax List:

Peter Guerrant District:

Proprietors Names	Quantity of Land	Value p Acre	Amount	1½ p Cent	Identification
Archibald Write	220	4/4	47.13.4	14.1½	1810 Archibald Wright of Buckingham County, son of 1774 George Wright of Cumberland County and grandson of 1769 George Wright of Essex County

Appendix: Buckingham County, Virginia, 1789 Land Tax List:

Josias Jones District:

Proprietors Names	Quantity of Land	Value p Acre	Amount	1½ p Cent	Identification
John Wright Sr	150	2/4	17.10.0	0.5.3	1809 John Wright of Buckingham County
John Wright Potter	285	8/4	47.10.0	0.14.2	1826 John Wright of Buckingham County
John Wright Jr	322	2/	32.4.0	0.9.7	John Wright, Jr., son of 1826 John Wright of Buckingham County
Thomas Wright (Amht)	400	2/4	46.13.4	0.14.0	

1790 LAND TAX LIST

BUCKINGHAM COUNTY, VIRGINIA

Appendix: Buckingham County, Virginia, 1790 Land Tax List:

Peter Guerrant District:

Proprietors Names	Quantity of Land	Value p Acre	Amount	1½ p Cent	Identification
Archibald Wright	220	4/4	47.13.4	14.1½	1810 Archibald Wright of Buckingham County, son of 1774 George Wright of Cumberland County and grandson of 1769 George Wright of Essex County

Appendix: Buckingham County, Virginia, 1790 Land Tax List:

Josias Jones District No. 2:

Proprietors Names	Quantity of Land	Value p Acre	Amount	1½ p Cent	Identification
John Wright Sen	150	2/4	17.10.0	0.5.3	1809 John Wright of Buckingham County
John Wright Potter	285	3/4	47.10.0	0.14.2	1826 John Wright of Buckingham County
John Wright Jun	322	2/	32.4.0	0.9.7	John Wright, Jr., son of 1826 John Wright of Buckingham County
Thomas Wright Amht	400	2/4	46.13.4	14.0	

1791 LAND TAX LIST

BUCKINGHAM COUNTY, VIRGINIA

Appendix: Buckingham County, Virginia, 1791 Land Tax List:

Peter Guerrant District No. 1:

Proprietors Names	Quantity of Land	Value per Acre	Amount	1½ p Ct	Identification
Archebald Wright	120	4/4	26.0.0	7.9	1810 Archibald Wright of Buckingham County, son of 1774 George Wright of Cumberland County and grandson of 1769 George Wright of Essex County

Appendix: Buckingham County, Virginia, 1791 Land Tax List:

Josias Jones District No. 2:

Proprietors Names	Quantity of Land	Value p Acre	Amount	1½ p Cent	Identification
John Wright Senr.	150	2/4	17.10.0	5.3	1809 John Wright of Buckingham County
John Wright (Potter)	285	3/4	47.10.0	14.2	1826 John Wright of Buckingham County
John Wright Jun	322	2/	32.4.0	9.7	John Wright, Jr., son of 1826 John Wright of Buckingham County
Thomas Wright (Amherst)	400	2/4	46.13.4	14.0	

1792 LAND TAX LIST

BUCKINGHAM COUNTY, VIRGINIA

Appendix: Buckingham County, Virginia, 1792 Land Tax List:

Peter Guerrant District No. 1:

Proprietors Names	Quantity of Land	Value pr Acre	Amount	1½ per Cen	Identification
Archd Wright	120	4/4	26.0.0	7.9	1810 Archibald Wright of Buckingham County, son of 1774 George Wright of Cumberland County and grandson of 1769 George Wright of Essex County

Appendix: Buckingham County, Virginia, 1792 Land Tax List:

Josiah Jones District No. 2:

Proprietors Names	Quantity of Land	Value p Acre	Amount	1½ p Cent	Identification
John Wright Sen	150	2/4	17.10.0	5.3	1809 John Wright of Buckingham County
John Wright (Potter)	285	3/4	47.10.0	0.4.2	1826 John Wright of Buckingham County
John Wright Jun	322	2/	32.4.0	9.7	John Wright, Jr., son of 1826 John Wright of Buckingham County
Thomas Wright (Amherst)	400	2/4	46.13.4	14.0	

1793 LAND TAX LIST

BUCKINGHAM COUNTY, VIRGINIA

Appendix: Buckingham County, Virginia, 1793 Land Tax List:

Peter Guerrant District No. 1:

Proprietors Names	Quantity of Land	Value per Acre	Amount	1½ per Cent	Identification
Archibald Wright	120	4/4	26.0.0	7.9	1810 Archibald Wright of Buckingham County, son of 1774 George Wright of Cumberland County and grandson of 1769 George Wright of Essex County
Gabriel Wright	126	8/.	50.8.0	15.2	1807 Gabriel Wright of Buckingham County, son of 1774 George Wright of Cumberland County and grandson of 1769 George Wright of Essex County

Appendix: Buckingham County, Virginia, 1793 Land Tax List:

Josias Jones District No. 2:

Proprietors Names	Quantity of Land	Value p Acre	Amount	1½ p Cent	Identification
John Wright Sen	150	2/4	17.10.0	5.3	1809 John Wright of Buckingham County
John Wright (Potter)	285	3/4	47.10.0	0.14.2	1826 John Wright of Buckingham County
John Wright Jun	322	2/	32.4.0	9.7	John Wright, Jr., son of 1826 John Wright of Buckingham County
Thomas Wright (Amherst)	400	2/4	46.13.4	14.0	

1794 LAND TAX LIST

BUCKINGHAM COUNTY, VIRGINIA

Appendix: Buckingham County, Virginia, 1794 Land Tax List:

Peter Guerrant District No. 1:

Proprietors Names	Quantity of Land	Value p Acre	Amount	1½ per Cent	Identification
Archibald Wright	292½	8/-	117.0.0	1.12.1	1810 Archibald Wright of Buckingham County, son of 1774 George Wright of Cumberland County and grandson of 1769 George Wright of Essex County
Gabrial Wright	292	6/-	87.12.-	1.6.3	1807 Gabriel Wright of Buckingham County, son of 1774 George Wright of Cumberland County and grandson of 1769 George Wright of Essex County

Appendix: Buckingham County, Virginia, 1794 Land Tax List:

Josias Jones District No. 2:

Proprietors Names	Quantity of Land	Value p Acre	Amount	1½ p Cent	Identification
John Wright Sen	150	2/4	17.10.0	0.5.3	1809 John Wright of Buckingham County
John Wright (P)	285	3/4	47.10.0	0.14.2	1826 John Wright of Buckingham County
Thomas Wright (Amht)	400	2/4	46.13.4	0.14.0	

1795 LAND TAX LIST

BUCKINGHAM COUNTY, VIRGINIA

Appendix: Buckingham County, Virginia, 1795 Land Tax List:

Anthony Debrill District No. 1:

Proprietors Names	Quantity of Land	Value p Acre	Amount	1½ p Cent	Identification
Archibald Wright	292½	8/-	117.-.-	1.12.1	1810 Archibald Wright of Buckingham County, son of 1774 George Wright of Cumberland County and grandson of 1769 George Wright of Essex County
Gabriel Wright	292	6/-	87.12.-	1.6.3	1807 Gabriel Wright of Buckingham County, son of 1774 George Wright of Cumberland County and grandson of 1769 George Wright of Essex County

Appendix: Buckingham County, Virginia, 1795 Land Tax List:

Josias Jones District No. 2:

Proprietors Names	Quantity of Land	Value p Acre	Amount	1½ p Cent	Identification
Thomas Wright by Jno Wright	150	2/4	17.10.-	5.3	1812 Thomas Wright of Buckingham County, son of 1809 John Wright of Buckingham County
Tho Wrigh[t] (by Bell & Wright)	250	2/-	25.-.-	7.6	1842 Thomas Wright of Buckingham County, son of 1813 John Wright of Buckingham County and grandson of 1809 John Wright of Buckingham County
John Wright (B.C.)	285	3/4	47.10.-	14.2	1826 John Wright of Buckingham County
Thomas Wright (Amht)	400	2/4	46.13.4	14.-	

1796 LAND TAX LIST

BUCKINGHAM COUNTY, VIRGINIA

Appendix: Buckingham County, Virginia, 1796 Land Tax List:

Anthony Dibrell District No. 1:

Proprietors Names	No. of Acres	Value	Amount	1 & ½ p Cent	Identification
Archibald Wright	292½	8/-	117.-.-	1.12.1	1810 Archibald Wright of Buckingham County, son of 1774 George Wright of Cumberland County and grandson of 1769 George Wright of Essex County
Gabriel Wright	292	6/-	87.12.-	1.6.3	1807 Gabriel Wright of Buckingham County, son of 1774 George Wright of Cumberland County and grandson of 1769 George Wright of Essex County

Appendix: Buckingham County, Virginia, 1796 Land Tax List:

Josias Jones District No. 2:

Proprietors Names	Quantity of Land	Value p Acre	Amount	1½ p Cent	Identification
Thomas Wright junr.	150	2/4	17.10.-	5.3	1812 Thomas Wright of Buckingham County, son of 1809 John Wright of Buckingham County
Tho Wright p Bell & Wright	250	2/-	25.-.-	7.6	1842 Thomas Wright of Buckingham County, son of 1813 John Wright of Buckingham County and grandson of 1809 John Wright of Buckingham County
John Wright B. Creek	285	3/4	47.10.-	14.2	1826 John Wright of Buckingham County
Thomas Wright (Amht)	400	2/4	46.13.4	14.-	

1797 LAND TAX LIST

BUCKINGHAM COUNTY, VIRGINIA

Appendix: Buckingham County, Virginia, 1797 Land Tax List:

A. Dibrell District No. 1:

Proprietors Names	No. of Acres	Value	Amount	1½ p Cent	Identification
Archibald Wright	292½	8/-	117.-.-	1.12.1	1810 Archibald Wright of Buckingham County, son of 1774 George Wright of Cumberland County and grandson of 1769 George Wright of Essex County
Gabriel Wright	292	6/-	87.12.-	1.6.3	1807 Gabriel Wright of Buckingham County, son of 1774 George Wright of Cumberland County and grandson of 1769 George Wright of Essex County

Appendix: Buckingham County, Virginia, 1797 Land Tax List:

Josias Jones District No. 2:

Proprietors Names	Quantity of Land	Value p Acre	Amount	1½ p Cent	Identification
John Wright Jur	150	2/4	17.10.-	5.3	Possibly 1812 Thomas Wright of Buckingham County, son of 1809 John Wright of Buckingham County
Thos. Wright p Bell & Wright	250	2/-	25.0.0	7.6	1842 Thomas Wright of Buckingham County, son of 1813 John Wright of Buckingham County and grandson of 1809 John Wright of Buckingham County
John Wright (B. Creek)	285	3/4	47.10.-	14.2	1826 John Wright of Buckingham County
Thomas Wright (Amherst)	400	2/4	46.13.4	14.0	

1653(063025)

1798 LAND TAX LIST

BUCKINGHAM COUNTY, VIRGINIA

Appendix: Buckingham County, Virginia, 1798 Land Tax List:

A. Dibrell District No. 1:

Proprietors Names	Quantity of Land	Value p Acre	Amount	Amount of Taxes @ 38 Cents Dolls Cent	Identification
Archibald Wright	292½	8/-	117.-.-	1.48	1810 Archibald Wright of Buckingham County, son of
Ditto p Ransone	41½	7/5	15.7.9	.19	1774 George Wright of Cumberland County and grandson of 1769 George Wright of Essex County
Gabrial Wright	292	6/-	87.12.-	1.11	1807 Gabriel Wright of Buckingham County, son of 1774 George Wright of Cumberland County and grandson of 1769 George Wright of Essex County

Appendix: Buckingham County, Virginia, 1798 Land Tax List:

Josias Jones District No. 2:

Proprietors Names	Quantity of Land	Value p Acre	Amount	Dollars Cents Land @ 38 Cent	Identification
Thomas Wright Junr	150	2/4	17.170.-	.22	1812 Thomas Wright of Buckingham County, son of 1809 John Wright of Buckingham County
Thomas Wright (p B. & Wright)	250	2/-	26.6.6	.34	1842 Thomas Wright of Buckingham County, son of 1813 John Wright of Buckingham County and grandson of 1809 John Wright of Buckingham County
John Wright (B. C.)	285	3/4	47.10.-	.60	1826 John Wright of Buckingham County
Thomas Wright (Amherst)	400	2/4	46.13.4	.59	

1653(063025)

1799 LAND TAX LIST

BUCKINGHAM COUNTY, VIRGINIA

Appendix: Buckingham County, Virginia, 1799 Land Tax List:

A. Dibrell District No. 1:

Proprietors Names	Quantity of Land	Value p Acre	Add Valu- ation Amount	at 48 Cts. for $ Amot of tax $ Cts	Identification
Archibald Wright	292½	8/-	117.-.-	1.87	1810 Archibald Wright of Buckingham County, son of
Ditto p Ransone	41½	7/5	15.7.9	.24	1774 George Wright of Cumberland County and grandson of 1769 George Wright of Essex County
Gabriel Wright	292	6/-	87.12.0	1.40	1807 Gabriel Wright of Buckingham County, son of 1774 George Wright of Cumberland County and grandson of 1769 George Wright of Essex County

Appendix: Buckingham County, Virginia, 1799 Land Tax List:

Josias Jones District No. 2:

Proprietors Names	Quantity of Land	Value p Acre	Amount Add Valua- tion	Dollars Cents at 48 Cts for $10	Identification
Thomas Wright Jun	150	2/4	17.17.-	.28	1812 Thomas Wright of Buckingham County, son of 1809 John Wright of Buckingham County
Thomas Wright p B & Wright	250	2/	26.6.6	.42	1842 Thomas Wright of Buckingham County, son of 1813 John Wright of Buckingham County and grandson of 1809 John Wright of Buckingham County
John Wright (BC)	285	3/4	47.10.-	.76	1826 John Wright of Buckingham County
Thomas Wright (Amherst)	400	2/4	46.13.4	.74	

1800 LAND TAX LIST

BUCKINGHAM COUNTY, VIRGINIA

Appendix: Buckingham County, Virginia, 1800 Land Tax List:

A. Dibrell District No. 1:

Proprietors Names	Quantity of Land	Value	Amount	Amount of Revenue	Identification
Archibald Wright	292½	8/-	117.-.-	1.87	1810 Archibald Wright of Buckingham County, son of
Ditto p Ransone	41½	7/5	15.7.9	.24	1774 George Wright of Cumberland County and grandson of 1769 George Wright of Essex County
Gabriel Wright	292	6/-	87.12.-	1.40	1807 Gabriel Wright of Buckingham County, son of 1774 George Wright of Cumberland County and grandson of 1769 George Wright of Essex County

Appendix: Buckingham County, Virginia, 1800 Land Tax List:

Josias Jones District No. 2:

Proprietors Names	Quantity of Land	Value p Acre	Amount	Dollars Cents	Identification
Thomas Wright j	150	2/4	17.17.-	.28	1812 Thomas Wright of Buckingham County, son of
ditto pr Samuel McCormick	100	3/-	15.00	.24	1809 John Wright of Buckingham County
Thomas Wright pr B & Wright	250	2/0	26.0.0	.40	1842 Thomas Wright of Buckingham County, son of 1813 John Wright of Buckingham County and grandson of 1809 John Wright of Buckingham County
John Wright (BC)	285	3/4	47.10.0	.76	1826 John Wright of Buckingham County
ditto pr Rd Coleman	10	4/	2.0.0	.03	
Thomas Wright (Amherst)	400	2/4	46.13.4	.74	

1801 LAND TAX LIST

BUCKINGHAM COUNTY, VIRGINIA

Appendix: Buckingham County, Virginia, 1801 Land Tax List:

A. Dibrell District No. 1:

Proprietors Names	Quantity of Land	Value	Amount	Amt Revenue	Identification
Archibald Wright	292½	8/-	117.-.-	1.87	1810 Archibald Wright of Buckingham County, son of
Ditto	41½	7/5	15.7.9	.24	1774 George Wright of Cumberland County and grandson of 1769 George Wright of Essex County
Gabriel Wright	292	6/-	87.12.-	1.40	1807 Gabriel Wright of Buckingham County, son of 1774 George Wright of Cumberland County and grandson of 1769 George Wright of Essex County

Appendix: Buckingham County, Virginia, 1801 Land Tax List:

Josias Jones District No. 2:

Proprietors Names	Quantity of Land	Value p Acre	Amount	Dollars Cents	Identification
Thomas Wright Junr.	150	2/4	17.17.0	.28	1812 Thomas Wright of Buckingham County, son of
Ditto p S. McCormack	100	3/-	15.0.-	.24	1809 John Wright of Buckingham County
Thomas Wright	250	2/.	26.6.6	.40	1842 Thomas Wright of Buckingham County, son of 1813 John Wright of Buckingham County and grandson of 1809 John Wright of Buckingham County
John Wright (BC) p Miggin	285	3/4	47.10.-	.76	1826 John Wright of Buckingham County
ditto p R. Coleman	10	4/	2.0.-	.03	
Thomas Wright (Amherst)	400	2/4	46.13.4	.74	
Robert Wright p Gary	250	4/	50.0.-	.80	Probably 1809 Robert Wright of Patrick County, son of _____ Wright and Mary (_____) Wright
Robert Wright p C. Staples	25	3/0	3.15.-	.05	Probably 1809 Robert Wright of Patrick County, son of _____ Wright and Mary (_____) Wright

1802 LAND TAX LIST

BUCKINGHAM COUNTY, VIRGINIA

Appendix: Buckingham County, Virginia, 1802 Land Tax List:

A. Dibrell District No. 1:

Proprietors Names	Quantity of Land	Value p Acre	Amount	Amount Revenue	Identification
Archibald Wright	292½	8/-	117.-.-	1.87	1810 Archibald Wright of Buckingham County, son of
Ditto p Ransone	41½	7/5	15.7.9	.25	1774 George Wright of Cumberland County and grandson of 1769 George Wright of Essex County
Gabriel Wright	292	6/-	87.12.0	1.40	1807 Gabriel Wright of Buckingham County, son of 1774 George Wright of Cumberland County and grandson of 1769 George Wright of Essex County

Appendix: Buckingham County, Virginia, 1802 Land Tax List:

Josias Jones District No. 2:

Proprietors Names	Quantity of Land	Value p Acre	Amount	Dollars Cents	Identification
Thomas Wright Jun	150	2/6	17.17.-	.28	1812 Thomas Wright of Buckingham County, son of
Do p McCormick	100	3/-	15.-.-	.24	1809 John Wright of Buckingham County
Thomas Wright	250	2/.	25.-.-	.40	1842 Thomas Wright of Buckingham County, son of 1813 John Wright of Buckingham County and grandson of 1809 John Wright of Buckingham County
John Wright	195	3/4	32.10.-	.52	1826 John Wright of Buckingham County
Do p Coleman	10	4/	2.-.-	.03	
Thomas Wright (Amherst)	400	2/4	46.13.4	.74	
Robert Wright	250	4/	50.0.-	.80	Probably 1809 Robert Wright of Patrick County, son of ____ Wright and Mary (____) Wright
Robert Wright p Staples	25	3/0	3.15.-	.05	Probably 1809 Robert Wright of Patrick County, son of ____ Wright and Mary (____) Wright

1803 LAND TAX LIST

BUCKINGHAM COUNTY, VIRGINIA

Appendix: Buckingham County, Virginia, 1803 Land Tax List:

A. Dibrell District No. 1:

Proprietors Names	Quantity of Land	Value p Acre	Amount	Amount Revenue	Identification
Archibald Wright	292½	8/-	117.0.0	1.87	1810 Archibald Wright of Buckingham County, son of
Ditto	41½	7/5	15.7.9	.25	1774 George Wright of Cumberland County and grandson of 1769 George Wright of Essex County
Gabriel Wright	292	6/-	87.12.0	1.40	1807 Gabriel Wright of Buckingham County, son of 1774 George Wright of Cumberland County and grandson of 1769 George Wright of Essex County

Appendix: Buckingham County, Virginia, 1803 Land Tax List:

Josias Jones District No. 2:

Proprietors Names	Quantity of Land	Value p Acre	Amount	Dollars Cents	Identification
Thomas Wright Jur	150	2/6	17.17.0	.28	1812 Thomas Wright of Buckingham County, son of
Do p McCormick	100	3/-	15.-.-	.24	1809 John Wright of Buckingham County
Thomas Wright	250	2/.	25.0.0	.40	1842 Thomas Wright of Buckingham County, son of 1813 John Wright of Buckingham County and grandson of 1809 John Wright of Buckingham County
Jno Wright	195	3/4	32.10.0	.52	1826 John Wright of Buckingham County
Do p Coleman	10	4/	2.0.0	.03	
Thomas Wright (Amherst)	400	2/6	46.13.4	.74	
Robert Wright	250	4/	50.0.0	.80	Probably 1809 Robert Wright of Patrick County, son of _____ Wright and Mary (_____) Wright
Robert Wright p Staples	25	3/	3.15.0	.05	Probably 1809 Robert Wright of Patrick County, son of _____ Wright and Mary (_____) Wright

1804 LAND TAX LIST

BUCKINGHAM COUNTY, VIRGINIA

Appendix: Buckingham County, Virginia, 1804 Land Tax List:

A. Dibrell District No. 1:

Proprietors Names	Quantity of Land	Value p Acre	Amount	Amount Revenue	Identification
Archibald Wright	292½	8/-	117.-.-	1.87	1810 Archibald Wright of Buckingham County, son of
Ditto	41½	7/5	15.7.9	.25	1774 George Wright of Cumberland County and grandson of 1769 George Wright of Essex County
Gabriel Wright	292	6/-	87.12.0	1.40	1807 Gabriel Wright of Buckingham County, son of 1774 George Wright of Cumberland County and grandson of 1769 George Wright of Essex County

Appendix: Buckingham County, Virginia, 1804 Land Tax List:

Josias Jones District No. 2:

Proprietors Names	Quantity of Land	Value p Acre	Amount	Dollars Cents	Identification
Thos Wright jur	150	2/4	17.17.0	.28	1812 Thomas Wright of Buckingham County, son of
Do p McCormick	100	2/-	15.-.-	.24	1809 John Wright of Buckingham County
Thos Wright	250	2/.	25.-.-	.40	1842 Thomas Wright of Buckingham County, son of 1813 John Wright of Buckingham County and grandson of 1809 John Wright of Buckingham County
Jno Wright (B.C.)	195	3/4	32.10.-	.52	1826 John Wright of Buckingham County
Do p Coleman	10	4/.	2.-.-	.03	
Thos Wright (Amherst)	400	2/6	46.13.4	.74	
Robert Wright	250	4/	50.-.-	.80	Probably 1809 Robert Wright of Patrick County,
Do p Staples	25	3/	3.15.-	.05	son of _____ Wright and Mary (_____) Wright
Wm Wright (Land John B.C)	48	3/-	7.4	.12	William Wright, son of 1826 John Wright of Buckingham County
James Wright p coleman	109	6/	32.14	.53	1825 James Wright of Buckingham County, son of 1826 John Wright of Buckingham County

1805 LAND TAX LIST

BUCKINGHAM COUNTY, VIRGINIA

Appendix: Buckingham County, Virginia, 1805 Land Tax List:

A. Dibrell District No. 1:

Proprietors Names	Quantity of Land	Value p Acre	Amount	Amount Revenue	Identification
Archibald Wright	292½	8/-	117.0.0	1.87	1810 Archibald Wright of Buckingham County, son of
Ditto	41½	7/5	15.7.9	.25	1774 George Wright of Cumberland County and grandson of 1769 George Wright of Essex County
Gabriel Wright	292	6/-	87.12.0	1.40	1807 Gabriel Wright of Buckingham County, son of 1774 George Wright of Cumberland County and grandson of 1769 George Wright of Essex County

Appendix: Buckingham County, Virginia, 1805 Land Tax List:

Josias Jones District No. 2:

Proprietors Names	Quantity of Land	Value p Acre	Amount	Dollars Cents	Identification
Thomas Wright Junr	150	2/.	17.17.0	.28	1812 Thomas Wright of Buckingham County, son of
Do p M	100	3/.	15.0.-	.24	1809 John Wright of Buckingham County
Thomas Wright	250	2/.	25.0.0	.40	1842 Thomas Wright of Buckingham County, son of 1813 John Wright of Buckingham County and grandson of 1809 John Wright of Buckingham County
John Wright BC	107	3/4	17.6.8	.28	1826 John Wright of Buckingham County
Do p Phelps	50	6/.	15.0.0	.24	
James Wright p Wright	90	4/.	19.12.-	.34	1825 James Wright of Buckingham County, son of 1826
Do. p C	109	6/.	32.14.-	.53	John Wright of Buckingham County
Thomas Wright (Amherst)	400	2/6	46.13.1	.74	
Robert Wright	250	4/	50.0.-	.80	Probably 1809 Robert Wright of Patrick County,
Do p S	25	3/	3.15.-	.05	son of _____ Wright and Mary (_____) Wright
William Wright (son of Jno. BC)	48	3/.	30.0.-	.42	William Wright, son of 1826 John Wright of Buckingham County

1806 LAND TAX LIST

BUCKINGHAM COUNTY, VIRGINIA

Appendix: Buckingham County, Virginia, 1806 Land Tax List:

A. Dibrell District No. 1:

Proprietors Names	Quantity of Land	Value p Acre	Amount	Amount Revenue	Identification
Archibald Wright	292½	8/-	117.0.0	1.87	1810 Archibald Wright of Buckingham County, son of
Ditto p Ranso	41½	7/5	15.7.9	.25	1774 George Wright of Cumberland County and grandson of 1769 George Wright of Essex County
Gabriel Wright	292	6/-	87.12.0	1.40	1807 Gabriel Wright of Buckingham County, son of 1774 George Wright of Cumberland County and grandson of 1769 George Wright of Essex County

Appendix: Buckingham County, Virginia, 1806 Land Tax List:

Josias Jones District No. 2:

Proprietors Names	Quantity of Land	Value p Acre	Amount	Dollars Cents	Identification
Thomas Wright Junr	150	2/4	17.17.0	.28	1812 Thomas Wright of Buckingham County, son of
Do	100	3/	15.0.-	.24	1809 John Wright of Buckingham County
Thomas Wright	250	2/.	25.0.0	.40	1842 Thomas Wright of Buckingham County, son of
Do p N & Thos. Conner	249	3/.	37.7.-	.60	1813 John Wright of Buckingham County and grandson of 1809 John Wright of Buckingham County
John Wright (BC)	107	3/4	17.18.8	.28	1826 John Wright of Buckingham County
Do	50	6/.	15.0.-	.24	
James Wright	98	4/.	19.12.-	.31	1825 James Wright of Buckingham County, son of 1826
Do	109	6/.	32.14.-	.53	John Wright of Buckingham County
Thos Wright (Amherst)	400	2/6	46.13.1	.74	
Robert Wright	250	4/	50.0.-	.80	Probably 1809 Robert Wright of Patrick County, son of _____ Wright and Mary (_____) Wright
Wm Wright (son of Jno. BC)	48	3/.	7.4.-	.11	William Wright, son of 1826 John Wright of Buckingham County

1807 LAND TAX LIST

BUCKINGHAM COUNTY, VIRGINIA

Appendix: Buckingham County, Virginia, 1807 Land Tax List:

A. Dibrell District No. 1:

Proprietors Names	Quantity Land	Value p Acre	Amount	Amount Revenue	Identification
Archibald Wright	292½	8/	117.0.0	1.87	1810 Archibald Wright of Buckingham County, son of
Ditto p Ransone	41½	7/5	15.7.9	.25	1774 George Wright of Cumberland County and grandson of 1769 George Wright of Essex County
Gabriel Wright	292	6/	87.12.0	1.40	1807 Gabriel Wright of Buckingham County, son of 1774 George Wright of Cumberland County and grandson of 1769 George Wright of Essex County

Appendix: Buckingham County, Virginia, 1807 Land Tax List:

Josias Jones District No. 2:

Proprietors Names	Quantity of Land	Value p Acre	Amount	Dollars Cents	Identification
Thomas Wright Jur	150	2/4	17.17.	.28	1812 Thomas Wright of Buckingham County, son of
do do do	100	3/4	15.0.0	.24	1809 John Wright of Buckingham County
Thomas Wright	250	2/-	25.0.0	.46	1842 Thomas Wright of Buckingham County, son of
Do p Nicholas & Thomas Conner	249	3/-	37.7.0	.60	1813 John Wright of Buckingham County and grandson of 1809 John Wright of Buckingham County
John Wright (BC)	107	3/4	17.16.8	.28	1826 John Wright of Buckingham County
do do do	50	6/-	15.0.0	.24	
James Wright p W	98	4/-	19.12.-	.34	1825 James Wright of Buckingham County, son of 1826
do do do	109	6/-	32.14.-	.53	John Wright of Buckingham County
Thos Wright (Amherst)	400	2/4	46.13.1	.74	
Robert Wright	250	4/-	50.0.-	.80	Probably 1809 Robert Wright of Patrick County, son of _____ Wright and Mary (_____) Wright

1809 LAND TAX LIST

BUCKINGHAM COUNTY, VIRGINIA

Appendix: Buckingham County, Virginia, 1809 Land Tax List:

A. Dibrell District No. 1:

Proprietors Names	Quantity Land	Value p acre	Amount	Amount Revenue	Identification
Archibald Wright	292½	8/	117.-.-	1.87	1810 Archibald Wright of Buckingham County, son of
Ditto	41½	7/5	15.7.9	.25	1774 George Wright of Cumberland County and grandson of 1769 George Wright of Essex County
Gabriel Wright	292	6/	87.12.0	1.40	1807 Gabriel Wright of Buckingham County, son of 1774 George Wright of Cumberland County and grandson of 1769 George Wright of Essex County

Appendix: Buckingham County, Virginia, 1809 Land Tax List:

Josias Jones District No. 2:

Proprietors names	quantity of land	Value p Acre	Amount	dd Cents	Identification
Thomas Wright Senr	235	3/4	41.13.0	.65	1812 Thomas Wright of Buckingham County, son of
ditto ditto	101	3/6	17.15.6	.68	1809 John Wright of Buckingham County
Thomas Wright	250	2/	25.0.0	.40	1842 Thomas Wright of Buckingham County, son of
ditto pr Conners	249	3/	37.7.0	.60	1813 John Wright of Buckingham County and grandson
					of 1809 John Wright of Buckingham County
John Wright (BC)	50	6/-	15.0.0	.24	1826 John Wright of Buckingham County
James Wright	98	4/-	19.12.0	.31	1825 James Wright of Buckingham County, son of 1826
ditto	109	6/-	32.14.0	.53	John Wright of Buckingham County
ditto pr Wright	102	3/-	15.6.0	.25	
Thos Wright (Amherst)	400	2/4	46.13.1	.74	

1810 LAND TAX LIST

BUCKINGHAM COUNTY, VIRGINIA

Appendix: Buckingham County, Virginia, 1810 Land Tax List:

A. Dibrell District No. 1:

Proprietors Names	No. of Acres	Value p acre	Amount	Amot Revenue	Identification

[No Wrights listed]

Appendix: Buckingham County, Virginia, 1810 Land Tax List:

John T. Bocock District No. 2:

Proprietors Names		Quantity of land	Value p Acre	Amount	Revenue	Identification
Thomas Wright Senr		150	3/4	17.10.0	.28	1812 Thomas Wright of Buckingham County, son of 1809 John
ditto		100	3/	15.0.0	.24	Wright of Buckingham County
Thomas Wright		250	2/	25.0.0	.40	1842 Thomas Wright of Buckingham County, son of 1813 John
ditto p Conners		249	3/	37.7.0	.60	Wright of Buckingham County and grandson of 1809 John Wright of Buckingham County
John Wright Bent Creek		50	6/	15.0.0	.24	1826 John Wright of Buckingham County
James Wright		98	4/	19.12.0	.31	1825 James Wright of Buckingham County, son of 1826 John
ditto		109	6/	32.14.0	.52	Wright of Buckingham County
ditto p J Wright		102	3/	15.6.0	.25	
Thomas Wright (Amhst)		400	2/4	46.13.4	.75	
Catharine Wright	)	292	61.0	87.12.0	1.40	Catherine (Ransone) (Wright) Sharp, widow of 1807 Gabriel
Catharine Wright	)					Wright of Buckingham County, a son of 1774 George Wright of
Elizabeth Wright	)					Cumberland County and grandson of 1769 George Wright of
Flemsted R Wright	) p Winston	108	7/10	42.6.0	.68	Essex County and
George Wright	)					Children of 1807 Gabriel Wright of Buckingham County, grand-
Ambrose R. Wright	)					children of 1774 George Wright of Cumberland County and
Samuel Wright	)					great grandchildren of 1769 George Wright of Essex County
Catharine Wright	)					
Archibald Wright		292½	8/	117.0.0	1.87	1810 Archibald Wright of Buckingham County, son of 1774
ditto p Ransone		41½	7/5	15.7.9	.25	George Wright of Cumberland County and grandson of 1769 George Wright of Essex County

1653(063025)

1811 LAND TAX LIST

BUCKINGHAM COUNTY, VIRGINIA

Appendix: Buckingham County, Virginia, 1811 Land Tax List:

Anthony Dibrell District No. 1:

Proprietors Names	Quantity of Land	Value p Acre	Amount	Amot Revenue	Identification

[No Wrights listed]

Appendix: Buckingham County, Virginia, 1811 Land Tax List:

John T. Bocock District No. 2:

Proprietors Names		Quantity Land	Value p Acre	Amount	Ds Cts	Identification
Thomas Wright Senr		150	3/4	17.10.0	.28	1812 Thomas Wright of Buckingham County, son of 1809 John
do		100	3/	15.0.0	.24	Wright of Buckingham County
Thomas Wright		250	2/	25.0.0	.40	1842 Thomas Wright of Buckingham County, son of 1813 John
do p Conners		249	3/	37.7.0	.60	Wright of Buckingham County and grandson of 1809 John Wright of Buckingham County
John Wright BC		23	6/	6.18.0	.11	1826 John Wright of Buckingham County
Pryor Wright		27	6/	8.2.0	.13	1816 Pryor Wright of Buckingham County, son of 1826 John Wright of Buckingham County
James Wright		98	4/	19.12.0	.31	1825 James Wright of Buckingham County, son of 1826 John
do		109	6/	32.14.0	.52	Wright of Buckingham County
do		102	3/	15.6.0	.25	
Thomas Wright (Amhst)		400	2/4	46.13.4	.75	
Catharine Wright		260	6/	78.0.0	1.25	Catherine (Ransone) (Wright) Sharp, widow of 1807 Gabriel Wright of Buckingham County, a son of 1774 George Wright of Cumberland County and grandson of 1769 George Wright of Essex County
Elizabeth Wright	)					Children of 1807 Gabriel Wright of Buckingham County, grand-
Flemsted R Wright	)					children of 1774 George Wright of Cumberland County, and
George Wright	) p Winston	108	7/10	42.6.0	.68	great grandchildren of 1769 George Wright of Essex County
Ambrose R. Wright	)					
Samuel Wright	)				$20.48	
Catharine R Wright	)	28				
Archibald Wright Est		292½	8/	117.0.0	1.87	1810 Archibald Wright of Buckingham County, son of 1774
do p Ransone		41½	7/5	15.7.9	.25	George Wright of Cumberland County and grandson of 1769 George Wright of Essex County

Appendix: Buckingham County, Virginia, 1811 Land Tax List:

John T. Bocock District No. 2:

Proprietors Names	Quantity Land	Value p Acre	Amount	Ds Cts	Identification
Pryor Wright	27	6/	8.9.0	.13	1816 Pryor Wright of Buckingham County, son of 1826 John Wright of Buckingham County [Duplicate entry]

1812 LAND TAX LIST

BUCKINGHAM COUNTY, VIRGINIA

Appendix: Buckingham County, Virginia, 1812 Land Tax List:

Samuel Patteson District No. 1:

Proprietors Names	No. of Acres	Value p Acre	Amount	Amot of Reve.	Identification
Greene Wright	115½	6/-	34.13.-	.56	Nathaniel Green Wright of Smith County, Tennessee, son of 1831 Robert Wright of Smith County, Tennessee

Appendix: Buckingham County, Virginia, 1812 Land Tax List:

John T. Bocock District No. 2:

Proprietors		Quantity	Value p Acre	Amount	Dols Cts	Identification
Thomas Wright Senr		150	2/4	17.10.0	.28	1812 Thomas Wright of Buckingham County, son of 1809 John
Do		100	3/	15.0.0	.24	Wright of Buckingham County
Thomas Wright		250	2/	25.0.0	.40	1842 Thomas Wright of Buckingham County, son of 1813 John
Do p Conners		249	3/	37.7.0	.60	Wright of Buckingham County and grandson of 1809 John Wright
Do p Saml McCom'k		100	2/	10.0.0	.16	of Buckingham County
John Wright Bent Creek		23	6/	6.18.0	.11	1826 John Wright of Buckingham County
James Wright		98	4/	19.12.0	.31	1825 James Wright of Buckingham County, son of 1826 John
Do		109	6/	32.14.0	.52	Wright of Buckingham County
Do		102	3/	15.6.0	.25	
Thomas Wright (Amhst)		400	2/4	46.13.4	.75	
Catharine Wright		264	6/	78.0.0	1.25	Catherine (Ransone) (Wright) Sharp, widow of 1807 Gabriel Wright of Buckingham County, a son of 1774 George Wright of Cumberland County and grandson of 1769 George Wright of Essex County
Catharine Wright	)					Children of 1807 Gabriel Wright of Buckingham County, grand-
Elizabeth Wright	)					children of 1774 George Wright of Cumberland County, and
Flemsted R Wright	)					great grandchildren of 1769 George Wright of Essex County
George Wright	)	108	7/10	42.6.0	.68	
Ambrose R. Wright	)					
Saml. Wright	)					
Catharine R Wright	)					
Archibald Wright Est		292½	8/	117.0.0	1.87	Estate of 1810 Archibald Wright of Buckingham County, son of
Do p Ransone		41½	7/5	15.7.9	.25	1774 George Wright of Cumberland County and grandson of 1769 George Wright of Essex County

1813 LAND TAX LIST

BUCKINGHAM COUNTY, VIRGINIA

Appendix: Buckingham County, Virginia, 1813 Land Tax List:

Samuel Patteson District No. 1:

Proprietors Names	No. of Acres	Value p Acre	Amount	Amot of Revenue	Situation of the Land Designated &c	Identification
Green Wright	115½	6/-	34.13.-	.74	on Payne Creek his resd	Nathaniel Green Wright of Smith County, Tennessee, son of 1831 Robert Wright of Smith County, Tennessee

Appendix: Buckingham County, Virginia, 1813 Land Tax List:

John T. Bocock District No. 2:

Proprietors names	Designation	Quantity Land	rate p acre	Amount	Dols Cents	Identification
Catharine Wright	residence On Gillias Creek	96	7/6	36.0.0	.77	Catherine (Ransone) (Wright) Sharp, widow of 1807 Gabriel Wright of Buckingham County, a son of 1774 George Wright of Cumberland County and grandson of 1769 George Wright of Essex County
Catharine R. Wright	Adjoining ditto	42	6/	12.12.0	.27	Catherine R. (Wright) Clark, daughter of 1807 Gabriel Wright of Buckingham County, granddaughter of 1774 George Wright of Cumberland County, and great granddaughter of 1769 George Wright of Essex County
Samuel Wright	Do	25	7/10	9/13/__	.21	Samuel Wright, son of 1807 Gabriel Wright of Buckingham County, grandson of 1774 George Wright of Cumberland County, and great grandson of 1769 George Wright of Essex County
Ambrose R. Wright	Do	35	7/6	13.2.6	.18	Ambrose R. Wright, son of 1807 Gabriel Wright of Buckingham County, grandson of 1774 George Wright of Cumberland County, and great grandson of 1769 George Wright of Essex County
Thomas Wright	residence	250	3/4	41.13.6	.89	1842 Thomas Wright of Buckingham County, son of
Do p Conners	on Middle fork Slate river	249	3/	37.7.0	.80	1813 John Wright of Buckingham County and grandson
Do p McCormack	adjt Ro Moore & Others	100	2/	10.0.0	.22	of 1809 John Wright of Buckingham County
John Wright Bent Creek	His residence	126½	6/	37.19.0	.81	1826 John Wright of Buckingham County
Do p. Phelps	On the Mountain	50	3/	7.10.0	.16	
James Wright	residence Adjoining his Father	200	4/	40.0.0	.86	1825 James Wright of Buckingham County, son of 1826
Do	Adjoining Do	102	3/	15.6.0	.33	John Wright of Buckingham County

Appendix: Buckingham County, Virginia, 1813 Land Tax List:

John T. Bocock District No. 2:

Proprietors names	Designation	Quantity Land	rate p acre	Amount	Dols Cents	Identification
John Wright (S Jno)	adj. Tho. Wright & Jas. Doling	100	1/6	7.10.0	.16	1813 John Wright of Buckingham County, son of 1809 John Wright of Buckingham County
Archibald Wright Est	resd. Adj. T Lackland	292½	8/	117.0.0	2.50	Estate of 1810 Archibald Wright of Buckingham County,
Do	Bot. of Ransone	41½	7/5	15.7.9	.33	son of 1774 George Wright of Cumberland County and grandson of 1769 George Wright of Essex County
Thomas Wright	(Amherst)	400	2/4	46.13.4	1.00	

1814 LAND TAX LIST

BUCKINGHAM COUNTY, VIRGINIA

Appendix: Buckingham County, Virginia, 1814 Land Tax List:

Samuel Patteson District No. 1:

Proprietors Names	Residence	Estate	No. Acres	Discription	Distance & Bearing from the C. House	rate p acre	Amount	Amt. of Rev.	Alterations	Identification
Green Wright	Res.		115½	Paynes Creek	15 SE	6/	34.13.0	.98		Nathaniel Green Wright of Smith County, Tennessee, son of 1831 Robert Wright of Smith County, Tennessee

Appendix: Buckingham County, Virginia, 1814 Land Tax List:

Town of New Canton:

Proprietors	Residence	Estate	No. of Lots	Rate p Lot	Amount	Amot. Rev.	Identification

[No Wrights listed]

Appendix: Buckingham County, Virginia, 1814 Land Tax List:

John T. Bocock District No. 2:

Owners Names	Place of Residence	estate	No of Acres	Description	Distance & bearing from the C. House	rate p acre	Total Amt.	Dols Cts	Identification
Catharine Wright	A residt	for life	96	On Duckers Creek	18 S	7/6	36.0.0	1.02	Catherine (Ransone) (Wright) Sharp, widow of 1807 Gabriel Wright of Buckingham County, a son of 1774 George Wright of Cumberland County and grandson of 1769 George Wright of Essex County
Catharine R. Wright	Do	in fee	42	On Do Do		7/6	12.12.0	.36	Catherine R. (Wright) Clark, daughter of 1807 Gabriel Wright of Buckingham County, grandaughter of 1774 George Wright of Cumberland County, and great granddaughter of 1769 George Wright of Essex County
Samuel Wright	not known	Do	25	On Do Do adj		6/	9.15.6	.28	Samuel Wright, son of 1807 Gabriel Wright of Buckingham County, grandson of 1774 George Wright of Cumberland County, and great grandson of 1769 George Wright of Essex County
Ambrose R. Wright	Do	Do	35	On Do Do		7/10	9.15.6	.28	Ambrose R. Wright, son of 1807 Gabriel Wright of Buckingham County, grandson of 1774 George Wright of Cumberland County, and great grandson of 1769 George Wright of Essex County

Appendix: Buckingham County, Virginia, 1814 Land Tax List:

John T. Bocock District No. 2:

Owners Names	Place of Residence	estate	No of Acres	Description	Distance & bearing from the C. House	rate p acre	Total Amt.	Dols Cts	Identification
Thomas Wright	Do	Do	250	Residence	10 W	2/	25.0.0	.75	1842 Thomas Wright of
Do			249	On Middle fork S river	9 W	3/	37.7.0	1.06	Buckingham County, son of 1813
Do			100	adj Ro. Moore & others	11 W	7/	160.0.0	3.97	John Wright of Buckingham County and grandson of 1810 John Wright of Buckingham County
John Wright (Bent Creek)	Do	Do	126½	On Both Sides Bent Creek	20 W	6/	37.19.0	1.07	1826 John Wright of Buckingham
Do			50	On the Mountain p Phelps		3/	7.10.0	.21	County
James Wright	Do	Do	200	adj Jas Wright on p Phelps	20 W	4/	40.0.0	1.13	1825 James Wright of Buckingham County, son of 1826 John Wright of Buckingham County
John Wright est	Do	Do	100	On the North fork S. River	10 W	1/6	7.10.0	.21	Estate of 1813 John Wright of Buckingham County, son of 1809 John Wright of Buckingham County
Archibald Wright est	Do	Do	292½	Adj Lackland & Ransone	20 SE	8/	117.0.0	3.32	Estate of 1810 Archibald Wright of Buckingham County, son of
Do			41½	adj Do Do		7/5	15.7.9	.44	1774 George Wright of Cumberland County and grandson of 1769 George Wright of Essex County

1815 LAND TAX LIST

BUCKINGHAM COUNTY, VIRGINIA

Appendix: Buckingham County, Virginia, 1815 Land Tax List:

Samuel Patteson District No. 1:

Proprietors Names	Residence	Estate	No of Acres	Discription	Distance & Bearing from the C. H.	Rate p acre	Amount	Amt. of Reve. $ Cts	Alterations Since 1814	Identification
Green Wright	Res.		115½	Paynes Cr.	15 SE	6/	34.13.0	.98		Nathaniel Green Wright of Smith County, Tennessee, son of 1831 Robert Wright of Smith County, Tennessee

Appendix: Buckingham County, Virginia, 1815 Land Tax List:

John T Bocock District No. 2:

Proprietors Names	Residence	estate	No Acres	Description	Distance & bearing from the C. House	Rate p acre	Amount	Dols Cts	Alterations	Identification
Catharine Wright	a resid	for life	96	On Mayors Branch	18 S	7/6	36.0.0	1.02		Catherine (Ransone) (Wright) Sharp, widow of 1807 Gabriel Wright of Buckingham County, a son of 1774 George Wright of Cumberland County and grandson of 1769 George Wright of Essex County
Catharine R Wright		in fee	42	On Ditto Do	18 S	6/	12.12.0	.36		Catherine R. (Wright) Clark, daughter of 1807 Gabriel Wright of Buckingham County, granddaughter of 1774 George Wright of Cumberland County, and great granddaughter of 1769 George Wright of Essex County
Samuel Wright			25	On Do Do	18 S	7/10	9.15.6	.28		Samuel Wright, son of 1807 Gabriel Wright of Buckingham County, grandson of 1774 George Wright of Cumberland County and great grandson of 1769 George Wright of Essex County

Appendix: Buckingham County, Virginia, 1815 Land Tax List:

John T Bocock District No. 2:

Proprietors Names	Residence	estate	No Acres	Description	Distance & bearing from the C. House	Rate p acre	Amount	Dols Cts	Alterations	Identification
Ambrose R Wright			25	On Do Do	18 S	7/10	9.15.6	.28	erroneously 35 at 7/6	Ambrose R. Wright, son of 1807 Gabriel Wright of Buckingham County, grandson of 1774 George Wright of Cumberland County, and great grandson of 1769 George Wright of Essex County
Thomas Wright			250	On the Waters S River	10 W	2/	25.0.0	.75		1842 Thomas Wright of Buckingham County, son of 1813 John Wright of Buckingham County and grandson of John Wright of Buckingham County
Do			249	On the Middle fork Adj	9 W	3/	37.7.0	1.06		
Do			100	Adj Ro. Moore	11 W	2/	10.0.0	.28		
John Wright (BC)	Resid	in fee	126	On Bent Creek adj Smith	20 Miles W	6/	37.19.0	1.07		1826 John Wright of Buckingham County
Do			50	On the mountain adj		3/	7.10.0	.21		
James Wright			200	On Bent Creek adj Jno. Wright	20 W	4/	40.0.0	1.13		1825 James Wright of Buckingham County, son of John Wright of Buckingham County
John Wright est			100	On N fork S River	10 W	1/6	7.10.0	.21		Estate of 1813 John Wright of Buckingham County, son of 1809 John Wright of Buckingham County

Appendix: Buckingham County, Virginia, 1815 Land Tax List:

John T Bocock District No. 2:

Proprietors Names	Residence	estate	No Acres	Description	Distance & bearing from the C. House	Rate p acre	Amount	Dols Cts	Alterations	Identification
Archibald Wright est	residt		292½	Adj Lackland & Ransone	20 SE	8/	117.0.0	3.32		Estate of 1810 Archibald Wright of Buckingham County, son of 1774 George Wright of Cumberland County and grandson of 1769 George Wright of Essex County
Do			41½	Do		7/5	15.7.9	.44		
Thomas Wright	Amherst		400	.	.	2/4	46.13.4	1.32		

1816 LAND TAX LIST

BUCKINGHAM COUNTY, VIRGINIA

Appendix: Buckingham County, Virginia, 1816 Land Tax List:

Samuel Patteson District No. 1:

Persons names owning land in Dist No. 1st 1816	Residence	Estate	No of Acres	Discription	Distance & bearing from the Court House	Rate pr Acre	Amount	Reve. $ Cts	Alterations since the last year	Identification

[No Wrights listed]

Appendix: Buckingham County, Virginia, 1816 Land Tax List:

John T. Bocock District No. 2:

Proprietors Names	Residence	estate	No Acres	Description	Distance & bearing from the Ct House	Rate	Amount	Dols Cts	Alterations	Identification
Catharine Wright	residt.	for life	96	On Mayors Branch	18 Miles S	7/6	36.0.0	.90		Catherine (Ransone) (Wright) Sharp, widow of 1807 Gabriel Wright of Buckingham County, a son of 1774 George Wright of Cumberland County and grandson of 1769 George Wright of Essex County
Catharine R. Wright		in fee	42	On Do Adj. Do	18 S	6/	12.12.0	.32		Catherine R. (Wright) Clark, daughter of 1807 Gabriel Wright of Buckingham County, granddaughter of 1774 George Wright of Cumberland County, and great granddaughter of 1769 George Wright of Essex County
Samuel Wright			25	On Do		7/10	9.15.6	.24		Samuel Wright, son of 1807 Gabriel Wright of Buckingham County, grandson of 1774 George Wright of Cumberland County, and great grandson of 1769 George Wright of Essex County

Appendix: Buckingham County, Virginia, 1816 Land Tax List:

John T. Bocock District No. 2:

Proprietors Names	Residence	estate	No Acres	Description	Distance & bearing from the Ct House	Rate	Amount	Dols Cts	Alterations	Identification
Ambrose R. Wright			25	On Do Do		7/10	9.15.6	.24		Ambrose R. Wright, son of 1807 Gabriel Wright of Buckingham County, grandson of 1774 George Wright of Cumberland County, and great grandson of 1769 George Wright of Essex County
Thomas Wright			250	On the Waters S River	10 W	2/	25.0.0	.63		1842 Thomas Wright of Buckingham County, son of 1813 John Wright of Buckingham County and grandson of 1809 John Wright of Buckingham County
Do			249	On Do Adj. Do		3/	37.7.0	.93		
Do			100	Adj. Ro. Moore		2/	10.0.0	.25		
John Wright (Bent Creek)			126½	On Bent Creek	20 W	6/	37.19.0	.95		1826 John Wright of Buckingham County
Do			50	On the Mountain Adj		3/	7.10.0	.19		
James Wright			100	On Broad Branch	20 W	2/	10.0.0	.25	200 sold and Conveyed to Celia L Page 100 Bot & Convd. by Jno Baskerville	1825 James Wright of Buckingham County, son of John Wright of Buckingham County

Appendix: Buckingham County, Virginia, 1816 Land Tax List:

John T. Bocock District No. 2:

Proprietors Names	Residence	estate	No Acres	Description	Distance & bearing from the Ct House	Rate	Amount	Dols Cts	Alterations	Identification
John Wright est			100	On the N fork Slate River	10 W	1/6	7.10.0	.19		Estate of 1813 John Wright of Buckingham County, son of 1809 John Wright of Buckingham County
Archibald Wright est			292½	Adj Lackland & Ransone	20 SE	8/	117.0.0	.93		Estate of 1810 Archibald Wright of Buckingham
Do			41½	Bot. of Ransone		7/5	15.7.9	.39		County, son of 1774 George Wright of Cumberland County and grandson of 1769 George Wright of Essex County
Thomas Wright	Amherst		400			2/4	46.13.4	1.17		

1817 LAND TAX LIST

BUCKINGHAM COUNTY, VIRGINIA

Appendix: Buckingham County, Virginia, 1817 Land Tax List:

Samuel Patteson District No. 1:

Name of owners	Residence	Estate	No of Acres of Land	Discription of the Land	Distance & Bearing from the Ct. House	Rate of land p acre	Total Value on Amount of Land	Amount of Tax upon Land $ Cts	Explanation of altera-tions during the preced-ing year	Identification

[No Wrights listed]

Appendix: Buckingham County, Virginia, 1817 Land Tax List:

New Canton:

Proprietors Names	Residence	Estate	No. of Lots	Rate p lot	Amount	Amt. of Rev. $ Cts	Different Changes since last year	Identification

[No Wrights listed]

Appendix: Buckingham County, Virginia, 1817 Land Tax List:

John T. Bocock District No. 2:

Proprietors Names	Residence	est.	No. Acres	description	distance & bearing from the Co. House	Rate	Amount	Dols Cts	Alterations	Identification
Catharine Wright	resid't.	for life	96	On Mayors branch	18 Miles S	7/6	36.0.0	.90		Catherine (Ransone) (Wright) Sharp, widow of 1807 Gabriel Wright of Buckingham County, a son of 1774 George Wright of Cumberland County and grandson of 1769 George Wright of Essex County
Catharine R Wright		in fee	42	On Do Adj. Do	18 S	6/	12.12.0	.32		Catherine R. (Wright) Clark, daughter of 1807 Gabriel Wright of Buckingham County, granddaughter of 1774 George Wright of Cumberland County, and great grand-daughter of 1769 George Wright of Essex County
Samuel Wright			25	On Do Do	18 S	7/10	9.15.6	.24		Samuel Wright, son of 1807 Gabriel Wright of Buckingham County, grandson of 1774 George Wright of Cumberland County, and great grandson of 1769 George Wright of Essex County
Do			22½	Adj. Do p Ambrose Wright		7/6	8.16.5	.22	Convd by Ambrose R Wright	
Thomas Wright			250	On Slate River	10 W	2/	25.0.0	.63		1842 Thomas Wright of Buckingham County, son of 1813 John Wright of Buckingham County and grandson of 1809 John Wright of Buckingham County
Do			249	On Middle fork Do	9 W	3/	37.7.0	.93		
Do			100	Adj. Robert Moore	11 W	2/	10.0.0	.25		
Do			20	Do		3/	3.0.0	.08	Convd by Charles Maxey's exrs	

Appendix: Buckingham County, Virginia, 1817 Land Tax List:

John T. Bocock District No. 2:

Proprietors Names	Residence	est.	No. Acres	description	distance & bearing from the Co. House	Rate	Amount	Dols Cts	Alterations	Identification
John Wright (BC)			116½	On Bent Creek	20 W	6/	34.19.0	.88	10 Convd to Jeff Parish	1826 John Wright (Bent Creek, Buckingham County)
Do			50	On the Mountain Adj		3/	7.10.0	.19		
James Wright			100	On Broad Branch	20 W	2/	10.0.0	.25		1825 James Wright of Buckingham County, son of 1826 John Wright of Buckingham County
John Wright est			100	On the N fork S River	10 W	1/6	7.10.0	.19		Estate of 1813 John Wright of Buckingham County, son of 1809 John Wright of Buckingham County
Archibald Wright est			292½	Adj Lackland & Ransone	20 Miles SE	8/	117.0.0	2.93		Estate of 1810 Archibald Wright of Buckingham County, son of 1774 George Wright of Cumberland County and grandson of 1769 George Wright of Essex County
Do			41½	Adj Residence of Ransone		7/5	15.7.9	.39		

1818 LAND TAX LIST

BUCKINGHAM COUNTY, VIRGINIA

Appendix: Buckingham County, Virginia, 1818 Land Tax List:

Samuel Patteson District No. 1:

Proprietors Names	Residence	Est.	No of Acres	Discription &c	Distance & Bearing from the Court house	Rate p Acre	Amount	Amount of Revenue $ Cts	Alterations since the last year	Identification

[No Wrights listed]

Appendix: Buckingham County, Virginia, 1818 Land Tax List:

Samuel D. Williams District No. 2:

Proprietors Names	Residence	est.	No Acres	description	distance & bearing from the Co. House	Rate	Amount	Dols Cts	Alterations	Identification
Catharine Wright	resid't.	for life	96	On Mayors branch	18 Miles S	7/6	36.0.0	.90		Catherine (Ransone) (Wright) Sharp, widow of 1807 Gabriel Wright of Buckingham County, a son of 1774 George Wright of Cumberland County and grandson of 1769 George Wright of Essex County
Catharine R Wright		in fee	42	On Do Adj. Do	18 S	6/	12.12.0	.32		Catherine R. (Wright) Clark, daughter of 1807 Gabriel Wright of Buckingham County, granddaughter of 1774 George Wright of Cumberland County, and great granddaughter of 1769 George Wright of Essex County
Samuel Wright Do			25 22½	On Do Do Adj. Do p Ambrose Wright	18 S	7/10 7/6	9.15.6 8.16.5	.24 .22	Convd by Ambrose R Wright	Samuel Wright, son of 1807 Gabriel Wright of Buckingham County, grandson of 1774 George Wright of Cumberland County, and great grandson of 1769 George Wright of Essex County

Appendix: Buckingham County, Virginia, 1818 Land Tax List:

Samuel D. Williams District No. 2:

Proprietors Names	Residence	est.	No Acres	description	distance & bearing from the Co. House	Rate	Amount	Dols Cts	Alterations	Identification
Thomas Wright			250	On Slate River	10 W	2/	25.0.0	.63		1842 Thomas Wright of
Thomas Wright			249	On Middle fork Do	9 W	3/	37.7.0	.93		Buckingham County, son of
Do			100	Adj. Robert Moore	11 W	2/	10.0.0	.25		1813 John Wright of
Do			20	Do		3/	3.0.0	.08		Buckingham County and grandson of 1809 John Wright of Buckingham County
John Wright (BC)			116½	On Bent Creek	20 W	6/	34.19.0	.88		1826 John Wright of
Do			50	On the Mountain Adj		3/	7.10.0	.19		Buckingham County
James Wright			100	On Broad Branch	_3 W	2/	10.0.0	.25		1825 James Wright of Buckingham County, son of 1826 John Wright of Buckingham County
John Wright est			100	On the N fork S River	10 W	1/6	7.10.0	.19		Estate of 1813 John Wright of Buckingham County, son of 1809 John Wright of Buckingham County
Thomas Wright			400	.	.	2/4	46.14.4	1.17		

1819 LAND TAX LIST

BUCKINGHAM COUNTY, VIRGINIA

Appendix: Buckingham County, Virginia, 1819 Land Tax List:

Samuel Patteson District No. 1:

Proprietors Names	Residence	Estate	No of Acres	Discription &c	Distance & Bearing from the Court house	Rate p Acre	Amount	Amount of Revenue $ Cts	Alterations since the last year	Identification
[No Wrights listed]										

Appendix: Buckingham County, Virginia, 1819 Land Tax List:

Samuel D. Williams District No. 2:

Proprietors Names	Resid.	est.	No. Acres	Description	Distance & Bearing	Rate $ ¢	Amt. £ s d	Dol. Cts Dols Cts	Alterations	Identification
Catharine Wright	rest.	in fee	96	On Mayors Branch	18 Miles S	7.06	36.0.0	.90		Catherine (Ransone) (Wright) Sharp, widow of 1807 Gabriel Wright of Buckingham County, a son of 1774 George Wright of Cumberland County and grandson of 1769 George Wright of Essex County
Catharine R Wright			42	On ditto ditto	18 S	6.00	12.12.0	.32		Catherine R. (Wright) Clark, daughter of 1807 Gabriel Wright of Buckingham County, granddaughter of 1774 George Wright of Cumberland County, and great granddaughter of 1769 George Wright of Essex County
Samuel Wright			25	on ditto ditto	18 S	7.10	9.15.6	.24		Samuel Wright, son of 1807 Gabriel Wright of Buckingham County, grand-son of 1774 George Wright of Cumberland County, and great grandson of 1769 George Wright of Essex County
ditto ditto			22½	adj. ditto Wm Amb Wright		7.10	8.16.3	.22		
ditto ditto			53½	adm David Woodall	20 SE	5.10	15.12.1	.39	Conveyed by Susanna Woodall	
Thomas Wright			250	On Slate River	10 W	2.00	25.0.0	.63		1842 Thomas Wright of Buckingham County, son of 1813 John Wright of Buckingham County and grandson of 1809 John Wright of Buckingham County
ditto ditto			249	On Middle F S River	9 W	3.00	37.7.0	.93		
ditto ditto			100	adj. Ro. Moore	11 W	2.00	10.0.0	.25		
ditto ditto			20	adj ditto ditto		3.00	3.0.0	.08		
John Wright (BC)			116½	On Bent Creek	20 W	6.00	34.19.0	.88		1826 John Wright of Buckingham County
ditto ditto			50	adj on the Mont.		3.00	7.10.0	.19		
James Wright			100	On Broad Branch	20 W	2.00	10.0.0	.25		1825 James Wright of Buckingham County, son of 1826 John Wright of Buckingham County

Appendix: Buckingham County, Virginia, 1819 Land Tax List:

Samuel D. Williams District No. 2:

Proprietors Names	Resid.	est.	No. Acres	Description	Distance & Bearing	Rate $ ¢	Amt. £ s d	Dol. Cts Dols Cts	Alterations	Identification

Appendix: Buckingham County, Virginia, 1819 Land Tax List:

Samuel D. Williams District No. 2:

Proprietors Names	Resid. est.	No. Acres	Description	Distance & Bearing	Rate $ ¢	Amt. £ s d	Dol. Cts Dols Cts	Alterations	Identification
John Wright (est)		100	On N fork of River	10 W	1.06	7.10.0	.19		Estate of 1813 John Wright of Buckingham County, son of 1809 John Wright of Buckingham County
Thomas Wright		400			2.04	46.14.4	1.17		

1820 LAND TAX LIST

BUCKINGHAM COUNTY, VIRGINIA

Appendix: Buckingham County, Virginia, 1820 Land Tax List:

Samuel Patteson District No. 1:

Name of Owner	Residence	Number of Acres of land	Discription of the Land	Distance & Bearing from the C.H.	Value of Land per Acre Dols Cts	Sum added to the Land on Account of the Buildings Dols Cts	Total Value Dols Cts	Amt of Reve. Dols Cts	Remarks	Identification

[No Wrights listed]

Appendix: Buckingham County, Virginia, 1820 Land Tax List:

Samuel Patteson List of Town Lots:

Name of Owner	Resident	No of lots	No of lots in plan of Town	Value of lots Dols Cts	Sum added to the lot on account of the buildings Dols Cts	Name of the Town	Amt of Reve. Dols Cts	Remarks	Identification

[No Wrights listed]

Appendix: Buckingham County, Virginia, 1820 Land Tax List:

Samuel D. Williams District No. 2:

									Identification
John Wright (B Creek)	166½	On Bent Creek	20 W	6.00	300.00	999.00	1.25		1826 John Wright of Buckingham County
Catharine Wright	96	On Mayo's Branch	13 SE	13.00	750.00	1248.00	1.36		Catherine (Ransone) (Wright) Sharp, widow of 1807 Gabriel Wright of Buckingham County, a son of 1774 George Wright of Cumberland County and grandson of 1769 George Wright of Essex County
Catharine R Wright	42	On Appomattox	13 SE	8.00		336.00	.42		Catherine R. (Wright) Clark, daughter of 1807 Gabriel Wright of Buckingham County, granddaughter of 1774 George Wright of Cumberland County, and great grand-daughter of 1769 George Wright of Essex County
Samuel Wright ditto	47½ 53	On Appomattox	13 SE	10.00 7.00	100.00 100.00	475.00 371.00	.06 .47	Conveyed by ____	Samuel Wright, son of 1807 Gabriel Wright of Buckingham County, grandson of 1774 George Wright of Cumberland County, and great grandson of 1769 George Wright of Essex County

Appendix: Buckingham County, Virginia, 1820 Land Tax List:

Samuel D. Williams District No. 2:

											Identification
Archibald Wright (est)										Conveyed to Zadoch Lackland	Estate of 1810 Archibald Wright of Buckingham County, son of 1774 George Wright of Cumberland County and grandson of 1769 George Wright of Essex County
Thomas Wright		250	On Slate River	10 W	4.00	200.00	1000.00	1.25			1842 Thomas Wright of Buckingham County, son of 1813 John Wright of Buckingham County and grandson of 1809 John Wright of Buckingham County
ditto		249	On Middle F Slate River	9 W	6.00		1494.00	1.67			
ditto		120	Adj. Robert Moore	11 W	1.50		180.00	.23			
John Wright (est)	Resid	100	On Slate River	10 W	3.00		300.00	.38			Estate of 1813 John Wright of Buckingham County, son of 1809 John Wright of Buckingham County

1821 LAND TAX LIST

BUCKINGHAM COUNTY, VIRGINIA

Appendix: Buckingham County, Virginia, 1821 Land Tax List:

Samuel Patteson District No. 1:

Name of Owner	Residence	Estate whether held in fee simple for life &c	Number of Acres of Land	Discription of the Land	Bearing from the Court house	Value of the land per acre including the buildings	Sum added to the Land on acct. of buildings	Total Value of the land & buildings	Amount of Tax	Explanation of alterations during the preceding year	Identification

[No Wrights listed]

Appendix: Buckingham County, Virginia, 1821 Land Tax List:

Peter R. Patteson District No. 2:

Name of Owner	Residence	No. of Acres	Discription of the Land	Distance & bearing from the Court house	Value of Land p Acre includ- ing build- ings	Sum added to to the Land on account of Buildings	Total Value of the Land including Buildings	Amt of Tax in $ cts	Explanation of Alterations During The preceding year	Identification
John Wright (BC)	Resident	166½	On Bent creek	20 W	6.00	300.00	999.00	.90		1826 John Wright of Buckingham County
Catharine R Wright	Resident	42	On Appotox	18 SE	8.00		336.00	.31		Catherine R. (Wright) Clark, daughter of 1807 Gabriel Wright of Buckingham County, granddaughter of 1774 George Wright of Cumberland County, and great granddaughter of 1769 George Wright of Essex County
Catharine Wright	Resident	96	On Mayo's Branch	18 SE	13.00	750.00	1248.00	1.13		Catherine (Ransone) (Wright) Sharp, widow of 1807 Gabriel Wright of Buckingham County, a son of 1774 George Wright of Cumberland County and grandson of 1769 George Wright of Essex County
Samuel Wright ditto	Resident "	47½ 53	On Appomattox ditto	18 SE "	10.00 7.00	100.00 100.00	475.00 371.00	.43 .34		Samuel Wright, son of 1807 Gabriel Wright of Buckingham County, grandson of 1774 George Wright of Cumber-land County, and great grandson of 1769 George Wright of Essex County

Appendix: Buckingham County, Virginia, 1821 Land Tax List:

Peter R. Patteson District No. 2:

Name of Owner	Residence	No. of Acres	Discription of the Land	Distance & bearing from the Court house	Value of Land p Acre includ- ing build- ings	Sum added to to the Land on account of Buildings	Total Value of the Land including Buildings	Amt of Tax in $ cts	Explanation of Alterations During The preceding year	Identification
Thomas Wright	Resident	250	Slate River	10 W	4.00	200.00	1000.00	.90		1842 Thomas Wright of Buckingham County, son of 1813 John Wright of Buckingham County and grandson of 1809 John Wright of Buckingham County
ditto	"	249	Middle Slate River	9 "	6.00		1494.00	1.35		
ditto	"	120	Adj. Robt Moore	11 "	1.50		180.00	.17		
John Wright est	Resident	100	Slate River	10 W	3.00	50.00	300.00	.27		Estate of 1813 John Wright of Buckingham County, son of 1809 John Wright of Buckingham County

1822 LAND TAX LIST

BUCKINGHAM COUNTY, VIRGINIA

Appendix: Buckingham County, Virginia, 1822 Land Tax List:

Samuel Patteson District No. 1:

Name of Owner	Residence	No of Acres of Land	Discription of the Land	Distance and bearing from the Court house	Value of Land p Acre Dols Cts	Sum added to the land on account of buildings Dols Cts	Total Value Dols Cts	Revenue Dols Cts	Explanation of alterations during the preceding year	Identification

[No Wrights listed]

Appendix: Buckingham County, Virginia, 1822 Land Tax List:

Peter R. Patteson District No. 2:

Name of Owner	Their Residence	No. of Acres	Description of the Land	Distance & bearing from the Court house	Value of Land p Acre includ- ing build- ings	Sum added to to the Land on account of Buildings	Total Value of Land including buildings	Amount of tax	Explanation of alterations During the preceding year	Identification
John Wright (BC)	Resident	166½	Bent Creek	20 W	6.00	300.00	999.00	.90		1826 John Wright of Buckingham County
Catharine Wright	Resident	96	Mayo's branch	18 SE	13.00	750.00	1248.00	1.13		Catherine (Ransone) (Wright) Sharp, widow of 1807 Gabriel Wright of Buckingham County, a son of 1774 George Wright of Cumberland County and grandson of 1769 George Wright of Essex County
Catharine R Wright	Resident	42	Appomattox	18 SE	8.00		336.00	.31		Catherine R. (Wright) Clark, daughter of 1807 Gabriel Wright of Buckingham County, granddaughter of 1774 George Wright of Cumberland County, and great granddaughter of 1769 George Wright of Essex County
Samuel Wright ditto	Resident "	47½ 53	Appomattox "	18 SE "	10.00 7.00	100.00 100.00	475.00 371.00	.43 .34		Samuel Wright, son of 1807 Gabriel Wright of Buckingham County, grandson of 1774 George Wright of Cumber-land County and great grandson of 1769 George Wright of Essex County

Appendix: Buckingham County, Virginia, 1822 Land Tax List:

Peter R. Patteson District No. 2:

Name of Owner	Their Residence	No. of Acres	Description of the Land	Distance & bearing from the Court house	Value of Land p Acre including buildings	Sum added to to the Land on account of Buildings	Total Value of Land including buildings	Amount of tax	Explanation of alterations During the preceding year	Identification
Thomas Wright	Resdt	250	Slate River	10 W	4.00	200.00	1000.00	.90		1842 Thomas Wright of
ditto	"	249	" "	9 "	6.00		1494.00	1.35		Buckingham County, son of
ditto	"	120	Adj Robert Moore	11 "	1.50		180.00	.17		1813 John Wright of
										Buckingham County and
										grandson of 1809 John Wright
										of Buckingham County
John Wright Est	Resdt	100	Slate River	10 W	3.00	50.00	300.00	.27		Estate of 1813 John Wright of
										Buckingham County, son of
										1809 John Wright of
										Buckingham County

1823 LAND TAX LIST

BUCKINGHAM COUNTY, VIRGINIA

Appendix: Buckingham County, Virginia, 1823 Land Tax List:

Samuel Patteson District No. 1:

Name of Owner	Residence	Number of Acres of Land	Discription of the Land	Distance and bearing from the Court house	Value of the Land per Acre including buildings	Sum added to the land on account of the buildings	Total value of the land and Buildings	Amount of Revenue	Explanation of alterations during the preceding year	Identification

[No Wrights listed]

Appendix: Buckingham County, Virginia, 1823 Land Tax List:

Peter R. Patteson District No. 2:

Names of owners	Their Residence	Number of Acres	description of land	Distance and general bearing from Court house	Value of land per acre including Buildings	Sum added to to the land on account of buildings	Total Value of the land & buildings	Amount of the Tax in $ & Cts	Explanation of alterations during the preceding year	Identification
Catharine Wright	Resdt	96	Mayo's Branch	18 SE	13.00	750.00	1248.00	1.00		Catherine (Ransone) (Wright) Sharp, widow of 1807 Gabriel Wright of Buckingham County, a son of 1774 George Wright of Cumberland County and grandson of 1769 George Wright of Essex County
Catharine R Wright	Resdt	42	Appomattox	18 SE	8.00		336.00	.27		Catherine R. (Wright) Clark, daughter of 1807 Gabriel Wright of Buckingham County, granddaughter of 1774 George Wright of Cumberland County, and great granddaughter of 1769 George Wright of Essex County
Samuel Wright ditto	Resdt "	47½ 53	Appomattox "	18 SE "	10.00 7.00	100.00 100.00	475.00 371.00	.38 .30		Samuel Wright, son of 1807 Gabriel Wright of Buckingham County, grandson of 1774 George Wright of Cumber-land County, and great grandson of 1769 George Wright of Essex County
John Wright (Bt Cr)	Resdt	166½	Bent Creek	20 W	6.00	300.00	999.00	.80		1826 John Wright of Buckingham County

Appendix: Buckingham County, Virginia, 1823 Land Tax List:

Peter R. Patteson District No. 2:

Names of owners	Their Residence	Number of Acres	description of land	Distance and general bearing from Court house	Value of land per acre including Buildings	Sum added to to the land on account of buildings	Total Value of the land & buildings	Amount of the Tax in $ & Cts	Explanation of alterations during the preceding year	Identification
Thomas Wright	Resdt	250	Middle Sl Riv	10 W	4.00	200.00	1000.00	.80		1842 Thomas Wright of
ditto	"	249	" "	9 "	6.00		1494.00	1.20		Buckingham County, son of
ditto	"	120	Adj Rob. Moore	11 "	1.50		180.00	.15		1813 John Wright of
ditto	"	70	Wts. Sl River	10 "	2.50		175.00	.14	Convd. by Ben Woody, who was not Chd. with any ld. but ought to have been	Buckingham County and grandson of 1809 John Wright of Buckingham County
John Wright est	Resdt	100	Slate River	10 W	3.00	50.00	300.00	.24		Estate of 1813 John Wright of Buckingham County, son of 1809 John Wright of Buckingham County

1824 LAND TAX LIST

BUCKINGHAM COUNTY, VIRGINIA

Appendix: Buckingham County, Virginia, 1824 Land Tax List:

List A:

Name of Owner	Residence	Number of Acres of Land	Discription of the Land	Distance and Bearing from the Court house	Value of the Land per Acre in- cluding buildings	Sum added to the land on account of the buildings	Total value of the land and Build- ings	Amount of Revenue	Explanation of alterations during the preceding year	Identification

[No Wrights listed]

Appendix: Buckingham County, Virginia, 1824 Land Tax List:

Peter R. Patteson District No. 2:

Name of owner	Their Residence	Num- ber of Acres	Discription of land	Distance and General bearing from Court house	Value of land p acre includ- ing build- ings	Sum added to to the land on Account of Buildings	Total Value of the land & buildings	Amount of the Tax in $ Cents	Explanation of Alterations during the preceding year	Identification
John Wright (BC)	Resdt	166½	On Bent Creek	20 W	6.00	300.00	999.00	.80		1826 John Wright of Buckingham County
Catharine Wright	Resident	96	Mayo's Branch	18 SE	13.00	750.00	1248.00	1.00		Catherine (Ransone) (Wright) Sharp, widow of 1807 Gabriel Wright of Buckingham County, a son of 1774 George Wright of Cumberland County and grandson of 1769 George Wright of Essex County
Catharine R Wright	Resident	42	On Appomattox	18 SE	8.00		336.00	.27		Catherine R. (Wright) Clark, daughter of 1807 Gabriel Wright of Buckingham County, granddaughter of 1774 George Wright of Cumberland County, and great granddaughter of 1769 George Wright of Essex County
Samuel Wright ditto	Resident "	47½ 53	On Appomattox "	18 SE "	10.00 7.00	100.00 100.00	475.00 371.00	.38 .30		Samuel Wright, son of 1807 Gabriel Wright of Buckingham County, grandson of 1774 George Wright of Cumber-land County and great grandson of 1769 George Wright of Essex County

Appendix: Buckingham County, Virginia, 1824 Land Tax List:

Peter R. Patteson District No. 2:

Name of owner	Their Residence	Number of Acres	Discription of land	Distance and General bearing from Court house	Value of land p acre including buildings	Sum added to the land on Account of Buildings	Total Value of the land & buildings	Amount of the Tax in $ Cents	Explanation of Alterations during the preceding year	Identification
Thomas Wright	Resident	250	Ws Slate River	10 W	4.00	200.00	1000.00	.80		1842 Thomas Wright of Buckingham County, son of 1813 John Wright of Buckingham County and grandson of 1809 John Wright of Buckingham County
ditto	"	249	Middle fork ditto	9 "	6.00		1494.00	1.20		
ditto	"	120	Adj Robt Moore	11 "	1.50		180.00	.15		
ditto	"	70	Ws Slate River	10 "	2.50		175.00	.14	Convd from B Woody in 23	
ditto	"	292	Middle ditto	" "	4.00	100.00	1168.00	.94	Convd. by Commissioner in 1824 Formerly Claibourn Maxey	
John Wright est	Resident	100	Slate River	10 W	3.00	50.00	300.00	.24		Estate of 1813 John Wright of Buckingham County, son of 1809 John Wright of Buckingham County

1825 LAND TAX LIST

BUCKINGHAM COUNTY, VIRGINIA

Appendix: Buckingham County, Virginia, 1825 Land Tax List:

Samuel Patteson District No. 1:

Name of Owner	Residence	No of Acres	Discription of the Land	Distance and Bearing from the Court house	Value of the land per acre in- cluding Building	Sum added to the land on acct of the building	Total value of the Land & Build- ings	Amt of Reve.	Explanation of alterations during the preceding year	Identification
Wm Wright	Resdt.	50	Buffaloe Cr.	14 E	3.00		150.00	.12	Convd. by Wm Adcock fn(?)	1863 William Wright of Buckingham County, probably son of 1803 John Wright of Cumberland County, grandson of 1770 John Wright of Cumberland County, and great grandson of 1769 George Wright of Essex County

Appendix: Buckingham County, Virginia, 1825 Land Tax List:

Peter R. Patteson District No. 2:

Names of Owners	Their Residence	No of Acres	Discription of Land	Distance and General bearing from the Crt. house	Value of land includ-ing build-ings	Sum added to to the land on account of buildings	Total Value of land including buildings	Amount of the Tax in $ Cts	Explanation of Alterations during the preceding year	Identification
John Wright (Bt Creek)	Resident	166½	On Bent Creek	20 W	6.00	300.00	999.00	.80		1826 John Wright of Buckingham County
Catharine Wright	Resident	96	Mayo's Branch	18 SE	13.00	750.00	1248.00	1.00		Catherine (Ransone) (Wright) Sharp, widow of 1807 Gabriel Wright of Buckingham County, a son of 1774 George Wright of Cumberland County and grandson of 1769 George Wright of Essex County
Catharine R Wright	Resident	42	Appomattox	18 SE	8.00		336.00	.27		Catherine R. (Wright) Clark, daughter of 1807 Gabriel Wright of Buckingham County, granddaughter of 1774 George Wright of Cumberland County, and great granddaughter of 1769 George Wright of Essex County
Samuel Wright ditto	NR "	47½ 53	Appomattox "	18 SE "	10.00 7.00	100.00 100.00	475.00 371.00	.38 .30		Samuel Wright, son of 1807 Gabriel Wright of Buckingham County, grandson of 1774 George Wright of Cumber-land County and great grandson of 1769 George Wright of Essex County

Appendix: Buckingham County, Virginia, 1825 Land Tax List:

Peter R. Patteson District No. 2:

Names of Owners	Their Residence	No of Acres	Discription of Land	Distance and General bearing from the Crt. house	Value of land includ- ing build- ings	Sum added to to the land on account of buildings	Total Value of land including buildings	Amount of the Tax in $ Cts	Explanation of Alterations during the preceding year	Identification
Thomas Wright	Resident	250	Ws Slate River	10 W	4.00	200.00	1000.00	.80		1842 Thomas Wright of Buckingham County, son of 1813 John Wright of Buckingham County and grandson of 1809 John Wright of Buckingham County
ditto	"	249	Middle fork ditto	9 "	6.00		1494.00	1.20		
ditto	"	20	Adj Robert Moore	11 "	1.50		180.00	.05	100 being Convd to Robert Moore in 1825 I think it should take all the tract	
ditto	"	70	Ws Slate River	10 "	2.50		175.00	.14		
ditto	"	292	Middle fork ditto	" "	4.00	100.00	1168.00	.94	Formerly Claibourn Maxey's Est	
John Wright est	Resident	100	Slate River	10 W	3.00	50.00	300.00	.24		Estate of 1813 John Wright of Buckingham County, son of 1809 John Wright of Buckingham County

1826 LAND TAX LIST

BUCKINGHAM COUNTY, VIRGINIA

Appendix: Buckingham County, Virginia, 1826 Land Tax List:

Samuel Patteson District No. 1:

Name of Owner	Residence	No of Acres of Land	Discription of the Land	Distance and bearing from the Court house	Value of the land p acre	Sum added to the land on account of the Buildings	Total Value	Amt of Revenue $ Cts	Explanation of Alterations	Identification
Wm Wright	Residence	50	Buffaloe Cr.	14 E	3.00		150.00	.12		1863 William Wright of Buckingham County, probably son of 1803 John Wright of Cumberland County, grandson of 1770 John Wright of Cumberland County, and great grandson of 1769 George Wright of Essex County

Appendix: Buckingham County, Virginia, 1826 Land Tax List:

Peter R. Patteson District No. 2:

Name of Owner	Residence	Number of Acres	Discription of land	Distance and bearing from the court house	Value of land pr acre including buildings	Sum added to to the land on account of buildings	Total Value of the land including buildings	Amount of Tax	Explanation of alterations during the preceeding year	Identification
John Wright	Resident	166½	On Bent Creek	20 W	6.00	300.00	999.00	.80		1826 John Wright of Buckingham County
Catharine Wright	Resident	64	On Mayo's Branch	18 SE	13.00	750.00	832.00	.67	32 Convd by Saml Wright to Archer & Wm Gills supposed to come from this tract	Catherine (Ransone) (Wright) Sharp, widow of 1807 Gabriel Wright of Buckingham County, a son of 1774 George Wright of Cumberland County and grandson of 1769 George Wright of Essex County
Catharine R Wright	Resident	42	On Appomattox	18 SE	8.00		336.00	.27		Catherine R. (Wright) Clark, daughter of 1807 Gabriel Wright of Buckingham County, granddaughter of 1774 George Wright of Cumberland County, and great granddaughter of 1769 George Wright of Essex County
Samuel Wright	N R	47½	On Appomattox	14 SE	10.00				Convd to A & Wm Gills	Samuel Wright, son of 1807 Gabriel Wright of Buckingham County, grandson of 1774 George Wright of Cumberland County and great grandson of 1769 George Wright of Essex County
ditto	N R	53	"	"	7.00				Also Convd to the Gills' as above	

Appendix: Buckingham County, Virginia, 1826 Land Tax List:

Peter R. Patteson District No. 2:

Name of Owner	Residence	Number of Acres	Discription of land	Distance and bearing from the court house	Value of land pr acre including buildings	Sum added to to the land on account of buildings	Total Value of the land including buildings	Amount of Tax	Explanation of alterations during the preceeding year	Identification
Thomas Wright	Resident	250		10 W	4.00	200.00	1000.00	.80		1842 Thomas Wright of
ditto	"	249	On Ws. Slate River	9 "	6.00		1494.00	1.20		Buckingham County, son of
										1813 John Wright of
ditto	"	20	Adj Robt. Moore	11 "	1.50		30.00	.03		Buckingham County and
ditto	"	70	Ws. Slate River	10 "	2.55		175.00	1.49		grandson of 1809 John
ditto	"	292	Middle fork ditto	" "	4.00	100.00	1168.00	.94		Wright of Buckingham
										County
John Wright Est	Resident	100	On Slate River	10 W	3.00	50.00	300.00	.24		Estate of 1813 John Wright of
										Buckingham County, son of
										1809 John Wright of
										Buckingham County

1827 LAND TAX LIST

BUCKINGHAM COUNTY, VIRGINIA

Appendix: Buckingham County, Virginia, 1827 Land Tax List:

Samuel Patteson District:

Name of Owner	Residence	No. of Acres	Discription of the Land	Distance & Bearing from the Court house	Value of Land per Acre	Sum added to the Land on account of the Buildings	Total Value of land & Build-ings	Amt. of Revenue $ Cts	Explanation of Altera-tions since the last year	Identification
Wm Wright	Resdt.	50	Buffaloe Cr.	14 E	3.00		150.00	.12		1863 William Wright of Buckingham County, probably son of 1803 John Wright of Cumberland County, grandson of 1770 John Wright of Cumberland County, and great grandson of 1769 George Wright of Essex County

Appendix: Buckingham County, Virginia, 1827 Land Tax List:

Peter R. Patteson District:

Name of Owner	Their Residence	No of Acres	Description of land	Distance & General bearing from the Court House	Value of land pr acre includ- ing build- ings	Sum added to to the land on account of improvmts	Total Value of the land in- cluding improve- ments	Amount of tax in $ cts	Explanation of Alterations during the preceeding year	Identification
John Wright (Bent Creek	Resident	166½	On Bent Creek	20 W	6.00	300.00	.	.	Conv'd. by Wm W. Ferguson &c to A. White	1826 John Wright of Buckingham County
Catharine Wright	Resident	62	Mayo's Branch	18 SE	13.00		832.00	.44	32 conveyed to the Gills and I expect they should be charged to all	Catherine (Ransone) (Wright) Sharp, widow of 1807 Gabriel Wright of Buckingham County, a son of 1774 George Wright of Cumberland County and grandson of 1769 George Wright of Essex County
Catharine R Wright	Resident		Appomattox	18 SE	8.00		336.00	.29		Catherine R. (Wright) Clark, daughter of 1807 Gabriel Wright of Buckingham County, granddaughter of 1774 George Wright of Cumberland County, and great granddaughter of 1769 George Wright of Essex County
Thomas Wright	Resident	250	Ws Slate River	10 W	4.00	200.00	1000.00			1842 Thomas Wright of Buckingham County, son of 1813 John Wright of Buckingham County and grandson of 1809 John Wright of Buckingham County
Ditto	"	249	Middle fork Slate River	9 "	6.00		1494.00	1.20		
Ditto	"	20	Adj Robt Moore	11 "	1.50		30.00	.03		
Ditto	"	70	On Ws Slate river	10 "			175.00	.16		
Ditto	"	292	Middle fork Do	" "	4.00		1168.00	.94		

Appendix: Buckingham County, Virginia, 1827 Land Tax List:

Peter R. Patteson District:

Name of Owner	Their Residence	No of Acres	Description of land	Distance & General bearing from the Court House	Value of land pr acre includ- ing build- ings	Sum added to to the land on account of improvmts	Total Value of the land in- cluding improve- ments	Amount of tax in $ cts	Explanation of Alterations during the preceeding year	Identification
John Wright Est	Resident	100	On Slate River	10 W	3.00	50.00	300.00	.24		Estate of 1813 John Wright of Buckingham County, son of 1809 John Wright of Buckingham County

1828 LAND TAX LIST

BUCKINGHAM COUNTY, VIRGINIA

Appendix: Buckingham County, Virginia, 1828 Land Tax List:

Samuel Patteson District:

Name of Owner	Residence	No. of Acres	Discription of the Land	Distance & Bearing from the Court house	Value of Land per Acre	Sum added to the land on account of the buildings	Total Value of land & Build-ings	Amt. of Revenue $ Cts	Explanation of altera-tions Since the last year	Identification
Wm Wright	Resdt.	50	Buffaloe Cr.	14 E	3.00		150.00	.12		1863 William Wright of Buckingham County, probably son of 1803 John Wright of Cumberland County, grandson of 1770 John Wright of Cumberland County, and great grandson of 1769 George Wright of Essex County

Appendix: Buckingham County, Virginia, 1828 Land Tax List:

Peter R. Patteson District:

Name of Owner	Their Residence	No of Acres	Discription of Land	Distance & general bearing	Value of lands including buildings	Sum added to to the land on acc't of buildings	Total Amount of the land and buildings	Amount of tax in $ cts	Explanation of alterations during the preceding year	Identification
John Wright (BC)	Resident	166½	Bent Crk	20 W					Convd. by William W Ferguson &c to A White in 1827	1826 John Wright of Buckingham County
Catharine Wright	Resident	62	Mayo's Branch						convd __	Catherine (Ransone) (Wright) Sharp, widow of 1807 Gabriel Wright of Buckingham County, a son of 1774 George Wright of Cumberland County and grandson of 1769 George Wright of Essex County
Catharine R Wright	Resident	42	Appomattox						____	Catherine R. (Wright) Clark, daughter of 1807 Gabriel Wright of Buckingham County, granddaughter of 1774 George Wright of Cumberland County, and great granddaughter of 1769 George Wright of Essex County

Appendix: Buckingham County, Virginia, 1828 Land Tax List:

Peter R. Patteson District:

Name of Owner	Their Residence	No of Acres	Discription of Land	Distance & general bearing	Value of lands including buildings	Sum added to to the land on acc't of buildings	Total Amount of the land and buildings	Amount of tax in $ cts	Explanation of alterations during the preceding year	Identification
Thomas Wright	Resident	250	Middle Slate River	10 W	4.00	200.00	1000.00	.80		1842 Thomas Wright of
do	"	249	do	9 "	6.00		1494.00	1.20		Buckingham County, son of
do	"	20	Adj Robt Moore	11 "	1.50		30.00	.03		1813 John Wright of
do	"	70	On Wts Slate River	10 "	2.50		175.00	.16		Buckingham County and grandson of 1809 John
do	"	292	" middle fork do	" "	4.00	100.00	1168.00	.94		Wright of Buckingham County
John Wright's Est	Resident	100	On Slate River	10 W	3.00	50.00	300.00	.24		Estate of 1813 John Wright of Buckingham County, son of 1809 John Wright of Buckingham County

1829 LAND TAX LIST

BUCKINGHAM COUNTY, VIRGINIA

Appendix: Buckingham County, Virginia, 1829 Land Tax List:

Samuel Patteson District:

Name of Owner	Residence	No. of Acres	Discription of the Land	Distance & Bearing from the Court house	Value of the land p acre in- cluding Building $ Cts	Sum added to the land on account of build- ings $ Cts	Total Value of the land & Build- ings $ Cts	Amt. of Tax $ Cts	Explanation of Altera- tions during the preced- ing year	Identification
Wm Wright	Resdt.	50	Buffaloe Cr.	14 E	3.00		150.00	.12		1863 William Wright of Buckingham County, probably son of 1803 John Wright of Cumberland County, grandson of 1770 John Wright of Cumberland County, and great grandson of 1769 George Wright of Essex County
ditto	"	95	"		3.00	20.00	285.00	.23	Convd. by Wm. Adcock jr	

Appendix: Buckingham County, Virginia, 1829 Land Tax List:

Peter R. Patteson District:

Name of Owner	Residence	No of Acres	Discription of the land	Distance and bearing from the Court-house	Value of land per acre includ-ing build-ings	Sum added on account of buildings	Total Value of land and buildings	Amount of tax in $ cents	Explanation of alterations during the preceeding year	Identification
Thomas Wright	Residt.	250	Middle Slate Riv	10 SW	4.00	200.00	1000.00	.80		1842 Thomas Wright of
ditto	"	249	" "	9 "	6.00		1494.00	1.20		Buckingham County, son of
ditto	"	20	Adj Robt Moore	11 "	1.50		30.00	.03		1813 John Wright of
ditto	"	70	Ws Slate River	10 "	2.50		175.00	.14		Buckingham County and
ditto	"	292	Middle fork	" "	4.00	100.00	1168.00	.94		grandson of 1809 John Wright of Buckingham County
John Wright Est	Residt	100	Slate River	10 SW	3.00	50.00	300.00	.24		Estate of 1813 John Wright of Buckingham County, son of 1809 John Wright of Buckingham County

1830 LAND TAX LIST

BUCKINGHAM COUNTY, VIRGINIA

Appendix: Buckingham County, Virginia, 1830 Land Tax List:

Samuel Patteson District:

Name of Owner	his Residence	No. of Acres	Discription of the Land	Distance & Bearing from the Court house	Value of the land p acre	Sum added to the Land on account of the buildings	Total Value	Amt. of Revenue $ Cts	Explanation of Altera- tions since the last year	Identification
Wm Wright	Resdt.	50	Buffaloe Cr.	14 E	3.00		150.00	.12		1863 William Wright of Buckingham County, probably son of 1803 John Wright of Cumberland County, grandson of 1770 John Wright of Cumberland County, and great grandson of 1769 George Wright of Essex County
ditto	"	95	"	"	3.00	20.00	285.00	.23		

Appendix: Buckingham County, Virginia, 1830 Land Tax List:

Peter R. Patteson District:

Name of Owner	Residence	No of Acres	Description of the land	Distance and general bearing from the C House	Value of land pr acre including buildings	Sum added to the land on account of buildings	Total value of land and buildings	Amount of Tax in $ Cts	Explanation of alterations during the preceeding year	Identification
Thomas Wright	Resident	250	On Mdl S River	10 SW	4.00	200.00	1000.00	.80		1842 Thomas Wright of
do	"	249	" "	9 "	6.00		1494.00	1.20		Buckingham County, son of
do	"	20	Adj R Moore	11 "	1.50		30.00	.03		1813 John Wright of
do	"	70	On Ws Slate River	10 "	2.50		175.00	.14		Buckingham County and grandson of 1809 John Wright
do	"	292	" Middle fork	" "	4.00	100.00	1168.00	.94		of Buckingham County
John's Wright Est	Residt	100	On Slate River	10 SW	3.00	50.00	300.00	.24		Estate of 1813 John Wright of Buckingham County, son of 1809 John Wright of Buckingham County
Roland Wright	Resident	100	On Ws Holliday	15 SW	.50	.	.50	.04		

1653(063025)

1831 LAND TAX LIST

BUCKINGHAM COUNTY, VIRGINIA

Appendix: Buckingham County, Virginia, 1831 Land Tax List:

Peter R. Patteson District No. 1:

Name of Owners	Residence	No. of Acres	Discription of the land	Distance and General bearing from the C. house	Value of the land per acre	Sum added to the land on Account of improve- ments	Total Value of the land including buildings	Amount of Revenue in $ cts	Explanation of Altera- tions during the preced- ing year	Identification
Wm Wright		50	Buffaloe Cr.	14 E	3.00		150.00	.12		1863 William Wright of Buckingham County, probably son of 1803 John Wright of Cumberland County, grandson of 1770 John Wright of Cumberland County, and great grandson of 1769 George Wright of Essex County
ditto		95	"	"	3.00	20.00	285.00	.23		

Appendix: Buckingham County, Virginia, 1831 Land Tax List:

District of John T. Bocock:

Name of Owner	Residence	No Acres	Description of the land	distance & bearing from the Cot House	Value p acre	Value of buildg	Total value of land & Builds	Revenue Ds Cents	Explanation of Alterations during the preceeding year	Identification
Thomas Wright	residt	250	Ws. Middle Slate R	10 SW	4.00	600.00	1000.00	.80		1842 Thomas Wright of Buckingham County, son of
Do	"	249	Same	9 "	6.00		1494.00	1.20		1813 John Wright of
Do	"	20	Adj Ro. Moore	11 SW	1.50		30.00	.03		Buckingham County and
Do	"	70	Ws Slate River	10 SW	2.50		175.00	.14		grandson of 1809 John Wright
Do	"	292	Middle fork Do	" "	4.00	100.00	1168.00	.94		of Buckingham County
John Wright est	Residt	100	Slate River	10 SW	3.00	50.00	300.00	.24		Estate of 1813 John Wright of Buckingham County, son of 1809 John Wright of Buckingham County
Rowland Wright		100	Ws. Holliday	15 SW	.50		50.00	.04		

1832 LAND TAX LIST

BUCKINGHAM COUNTY, VIRGINIA

1653(063025)

197.

Name of owners	Residence	No. of Acres	Discription of the Land	Distance & bearing from the Court-house	Value of the Land pr acre $ cts	Sum added to the Land on account of buildings	Total Value $ cts	Amount of Tax $ cts	Explanation of altera-tions since the last year	Identification
William Wright		50	Buffaloe Cr.	14 E	3.00		150.00	.12		1863 William Wright of Buckingham County, probably son of 1803 John Wright of Cumberland County, grandson of 1770 John Wright of Cumberland County, and great grandson of 1769 George Wright of Essex County
Do		95	"	"	3.00	20.00	285.00	.23		

Appendix: Buckingham County, Virginia, 1832 Land Tax List:

District of John T. Bocock District No. 2:

Name of Owner	Residence	No of Acres	Description of the land	distance & bearing	Value p acre	Value of buildings	Total Value	Tax Dls Cents	Alterations during present year	Identification
Thomas Wright	Residt.	250	Middle Slate Rv	10 SW	4.00	600.00	1000.00	.80		1842 Thomas Wright of
Do	"	249	On Same	9 "	6.00		1494.00	1.20		Buckingham County, son of
Do	"	20	Adj Same		1.50		30.00	.03		1813 John Wright of
Do	"	70	Ws Same		2.50		175.00	.14		Buckingham County and
Do	"	292	Middle Fork		4.00	100.00	1168.00	.94		grandson of 1809 John Wright of Buckingham County
John Wright est		100	Slate River	10 SW	3.00	50.00	300.00	.24		Estate of 1813 John Wright of Buckingham County, son of 1809 John Wright of Buckingham County
Rowland Wright		100	Ws. Slate River	15 SW	.50		50.00	.04		

1833 LAND TAX LIST

BUCKINGHAM COUNTY, VIRGINIA

Appendix: Buckingham County, Virginia, 1833 Land Tax List:

Peter R. Patteson District No. 1:

Owners Names	Residence	No. of Acres	Discription of the Land	Distance and Bearing from C.H.	Value of Land pr Acre $ cts	Sum added for Improve- ments $ cts	Total Value $ cts	Amount of Rev- enue in $ cts	Explanation of altera- tions &c	Identification
William Wright		50	Buffaloe Cr.	14 E	3.00		150.00	.12		1863 William Wright of Buckingham County, probably son of 1803 John Wright of Cumberland County, grandson of 1770 John Wright of Cumberland County, and great grandson of 1769 George Wright of Essex County
Do		95	"	"	3.00	20.00	285.00	.23		

Appendix: Buckingham County, Virginia, 1833 Land Tax List:

District of John T. Bocock District No. 2:

Name of the Owner	Resid.ce	No of Acres	discription of the land	distance & bearing	Value p Acre	Value of buildings	Total Value	Tax Dls Cents	Alterations during the last year	Identification
Thomas Wright	Resdt.	250	Middle Slate Riv.	10 SW	4.00	600.00	1000.00	.80		1842 Thomas Wright of
Do		249	On Same	9 SW	6.00		1494.00	1.20		Buckingham County, son of
Do		20	Adj Same	11 "	1.50		30.00	.03		1813 John Wright of
Do		70	Ws Same	10 "	2.50		175.00	.14		Buckingham County and
Do		292	Middle fork		4.00	100.00	1168.00	.94		grandson of 1809 John Wright of Buckingham County
John Wright's Est		100	Slate River	10 SW	3.00	50.00	300.00	.24		Estate of 1813 John Wright of Buckingham County, son of 1809 John Wright of Buckingham County

1834 LAND TAX LIST

BUCKINGHAM COUNTY, VIRGINIA

Appendix: Buckingham County, Virginia, 1834 Land Tax List:

Peter R. Patteson District No. 1:

Owners Names	Residence	No. of Acres	Discription of Land	Distance & bearing from the Court House	Value of Land pr Acre	Sum added for Improve-ments	Total Value in $ ¢	Amount of Rev-enue in $ ¢	Explanation of Altera-tions	Identification
William Wright		50	Buffaloe Cr	14 E	3.00		150.00	.12		1863 William Wright of Buckingham County, probably son of 1803 John Wright of Cumberland County, grandson of 1770 John Wright of Cumberland County, and great grandson of 1769 George Wright of Essex County
do		95	"	"	3.00	20.00	285.00	.23		

Appendix: Buckingham County, Virginia, 1834 Land Tax List:

John T Bocock District No. 2:

Name of the Owner	Residence	No of Acres	description of the Land	distance & bearing	Value p Acre	Value of Buildings	Total Value Build-ings in	Tax Dols Cts	Alterations since the last report	Identification
Thomas S. Wright		100	Slate River	10 SW	3.00	50.00	300.00	.24	Given by the last Will of John Wright	1883 Thomas Smith Wright of Campbell County, son of 1842 Thomas Wright of Buckingham County, grandson of 1813 John Wright of Buckingham County, and great grandson of 1809 John Wright of Buckingham County
Thomas Wright		250	Middle Slate Riv:	10 SW	4.00	600.00	1000.00	.80		1842 Thomas Wright of Buckingham County, son of
Do		249	On the same	"	6.00		1494.00	1.20		1813 John Wright of
Do		20	Adj Do	"	1.50		30.00	.03		Buckingham County and
Do		70	Adj. Do W. same	"	2.50		175.00	.14		grandson of 1809 John Wright
Do		292	Middle Fork	10 "	4.00	100.00	1168.00	.94		of Buckingham County

1835 LAND TAX LIST

BUCKINGHAM COUNTY, VIRGINIA

1653(063025)

..s Names	Residence	No. of Acres	Discription of Land	Distance & bearing from the Court House	Value of Land pr Acre	Sum added for Improve-ments	Total Value in $ ¢	Amount of Rev-enue in $ ¢	Explanation of Altera-tions	Identification
William Wright	Resdt	50	Buffaloe Cr	14 E	3.00		150.00	.12		1863 William Wright of Buckingham County, probably son of 1803 John Wright of Cumberland County, grandson of 1770 John Wright of Cumberland County, and great grandson of 1769 George Wright of Essex County
ditto	"	95	"	"	3.00	20.00	285.00	.23		

Appendix: Buckingham County, Virginia, 1835 Land Tax List:

District No 2:

Name of the owner	Residence	No of Acres		Distance & Bearing	Value p acre	Value of buildings	Total Value	Revenue	Explanation of altera- tions	Identification
Thomas S. Wright		100	Slate River	10 SW	3.00	50.00	300.00	.24		1883 Thomas S. Wright of Campbell County, son of 1842 Thomas Wright of Buckingham County, grandson of 1813 John Wright of Buckingham County, and great grandson of 1809 John Wright of Buckingham County
Thomas Wright		250	Middle Slate River	10 SW	4.00	600.00	1000.00	.80		1842 Thomas Wright of
Do		249	On the Same		6.00		1494.00	1.20		Buckingham County, son of
Do		20	Adj Same	11 SW	1.50		30.00	.03		1813 John Wright of
Do		70	Do Do		2.50		175.00	.14		Buckingham County and
Do		292	Middle fork		4.00	100.00	1168.00	.94		grandson of 1809 John Wright of Buckingham County

1836 LAND TAX LIST

BUCKINGHAM COUNTY, VIRGINIA

Appendix: Buckingham County, Virginia, 1836 Land Tax List:

Granderson Moseley District No. 1:

Name of Owner	Residence	No. of Acres	Description	Distance & Bearing from the Ct House	Rate per Acre	Value of Improvements	Value including Improvements	Revenue	Explanation &c	Identification
William Wright	Res	50	Buffalow Creek	14 E	3.00		150.00	.12		1863 William Wright of Buckingham County, probably son of 1803 John Wright of Cumberland County, grandson of 1770 John Wright of Cumberland County, and great grandson of 1769 George Wright of Essex County
Same		95	"	"	3.00	20.00	285.00	.23		

Appendix: Buckingham County, Virginia, 1836 Land Tax List:

John T Bocock District No. 2:

Name of the Owner	Residence	No. Acres	description of the land	distance & bearing from ye Cot House	rate p acre	Value of improve.ts	Total Value including improve- mt.s	Revenue Dols Cts	Alterations	Identification
Thomas S. Wright		100	Ws Slate River	10 SW	3.00	50.00	300.00	.24		1883 Thomas S. Wright of Campbell County, son of 1842 Thomas Wright of Buckingham County, grandson of 1813 John Wright of Buckingham County, and great grandson of 1809 John Wright of Buckingham County
Thomas Wright		250	Midl. Slate River	10 SW	4.00	600.00	1000.00	.80		1842 Thomas Wright of
Do		249	On Same		6.00		1494.00	1.20		Buckingham County, son of
Do		20	Adj Same		1.50		30.00	.03		1813 John Wright of
Do		70	On Same		2.50		175.00	.14		Buckingham County and
Do		292	Middle fork		4.00	100.00	1160.00	.94		grandson of 1809 John Wright of Buckingham County

1837 LAND TAX LIST

BUCKINGHAM COUNTY, VIRGINIA

Appendix: Buckingham County, Virginia, 1837 Land Tax List:

Granderson Moseley District No. 1:

Name of Owner	Residence	No. of Acres	Description	Distance & Bearing from the Ct House	Rate per Acre	Value of Improvements	Value including Improvements	Revenue	Explanation &c	Identification
William Wright		50	Buffalow	14 E	3.00		150.00	.12		1863 William Wright of
same		60			3.00	20.00	180.00	.14	5 to N MGhan	Buckingham County, probably
same		35			4.00		140.00	.12	from N MGhan	son of 1803 John Wright of Cumberland County, grandson of 1770 John Wright of Cumberland County, and great grandson of 1769 George Wright of Essex County

Appendix: Buckingham County, Virginia, 1837 Land Tax List:

John T Bocock District No. 2:

Name of the Owner	Residence	No. Acres	description of the land	distance & bearing from ye Cot House	rate p acre	Value of improve.ts	Total Value including improve- mt.s	Revenue Dols Cts	Alterations	Identification
Thomas S. Wright		100	Slate River	10 SW	3.00	50.00	300.00	.24		1883 Thomas S. Wright of Campbell County, son of 1842 Thomas Wright of Buckingham County, grandson of 1813 John Wright of Buckingham County, and great grandson of 1809 John Wright of Buckingham County
Thomas Wright		250	Middle Slate Riv:	10 SW	4.00	600.00	1000.00	.80		1842 Thomas Wright of
Do		249	On the Same		6.00		1494.00	1.20		Buckingham County , son of
Do		20	Adj Do		1.50		30.00	.03		1813 John Wright of
Do		70	Adj Same		2.50		175.00	.14		Buckingham County and
Do		292	Middle Fork		4.00	100.00	1160.00	.94		grandson of 1809 John Wright of Buckingham County

1653(063025)

1838 LAND TAX LIST

BUCKINGHAM COUNTY, VIRGINIA

Appendix: Buckingham County, Virginia, 1838 Land Tax List:

Granderson Moseley District No. 1:

Name of Owner	Residence	Number of Acres	Description	Distance and Bearing from Ct Hs	Rate per Acre	Value of Improve- ments	Total Value in- cluding Improve- ments	Revenue	Explanation of Altera- tions during 1837	Identification
William Wright		50	Buffalow	14 E	3.00		150.00	.15		1863 William Wright of Buckingham County, probably son of 1803 John Wright of Cumberland County, grandson of 1770 John Wright of Cumberland County, and great grandson of 1769 George Wright of Essex County
Same		60			3.00	20.00	180.00	.18		
Same		35			4.00		140.00	.14		

Appendix: Buckingham County, Virginia, 1838 Land Tax List:

John T Bocock District No. 2:

Name of Owner	Residence	No. Acres	discription	distance & bearing	Rate p Acre	Value of buildg	Total Value	Revenue	Alterations	Identification
Thomas S. Wright		100	Slate River	10 SW	3.00	50.00	300.00	.30		1883 Thomas S. Wright of Campbell County, son of 1842 Thomas Wright of Buckingham County, grandson of 1813 John Wright of Buckingham County, and great grandson of 1809 John Wright of Buckingham County
Thomas Wright		250	Middle S Riv	10 SW	4.00	600.00	1000.00	1.00		1842 Thomas Wright of Buckingham County, son of 1813 John Wright of Buckingham County and grandson of 1809 John Wright of Buckingham County
Do		249	On Same		6.00		1494.00	1.50		
Do		20	Adj Same		1.50		30.00	.03		
Do		70	On Same		2.50		175.00	.18		
Do		292	On same		4.00	100.00	1160.00	1.16		

1839 LAND TAX LIST

BUCKINGHAM COUNTY, VIRGINIA

Appendix: Buckingham County, Virginia, 1839 Land Tax List:

Granderson Moseley District No. 1:

Name of Owner	Residence	Number of Acres	Description	Distance and bearing from Ct Ho	Rate per Acre	Value of Improve-ments	Value in-cluding Improve-ments	Revenue	Explanation of Altera-tions during 1838	Identification
William Wright		50	Buffalo	14 E	3.00		150.00	.15		1863 William Wright of Buckingham County, probably son of 1803 John Wright of Cumberland County, grandson of 1770 John Wright of Cumberland County, and great grandson of 1769 George Wright of Essex County
Same		60			3.00	20.00	180.00	.18		
Same		35			4.00		140.00	.14		

Appendix: Buckingham County, Virginia, 1839 Land Tax List:

John T Bocock District No. 2:

Name of the Owner	resid.	No. of Acres	Description	distance & Bearing	rate p Acre	Value of improvms	Total Value	Total tax	Alterations since last report	Identification
Thomas S. Wright		100	Slate River	10 SW	3.00	50.00	300.00	.30		1883 Thomas S. Wright of Campbell County, son of 1842 Thomas Wright of Buckingham County, grandson of 1813 John Wright of Buckingham County, and great grandson of 1809 John Wright of Buckingham County
Thomas Wright		250	Middle Slate Riv	10 SW	4.00	600.00	1000.00	1.00		1842 Thomas Wright of Buckingham County, son of 1813 John Wright of Buckingham County and grandson of 1809 John Wright of Buckingham County
Do		249	On Same		6.00		1494.00	1.50		
Do		20	Adj Same		1.50		30.00	.03		
Do		70	On Same		2.50		175.00	.18		
Do		292	On same		4.00	100.00	1168.00	1.17		
Helena Wright		100	Ws Wreck Iland	29 W	7.00	100.00	700.00	.70	from Henry Baddow Nat Hood	Helena (____) Wright, wife of 1881 William P. Wright of Appomattox County, a son of Charles Wright and grandson of Robert Wright, Sr. (Campbell County)

1840 LAND TAX LIST

BUCKINGHAM COUNTY, VIRGINIA

Appendix: Buckingham County, Virginia, 1840 Land Tax List:

Charles Patteson District No. 1:

Owners Names	Residence	Kind of Estate	Discription or situation of the land	Distance & bearing from the Court House	Value of land pr acre including buildings	Sum added to the value of the land on act. of buildings	Total value of land and buildings	Revenue	Remarks	Identification
William Wright		50	Buffaloe	14 E	3.00		150.00	.15		1863 William Wright of
Same		60			3.00		180.00	.18		Buckingham County),
Same		35			3.00		105.00	.11		probably son of 1803 John
										Wright of Cumberland County,
										grandson of 1770 John Wright
										of Cumberland County, and
										great grandson of 1769
										George Wright of Essex
										County

Appendix: Buckingham County, Virginia, 1840 Land Tax List:

John T Bocock District No. 2:

Name of Owner	residence	kind of estate	No of Acres	description of the land	distance & bearing	rate p Acre Dols Cts	Value of improvms	total Value including buildings	Tax Dols Cts	Alterations since the Assessment	Identification
Thomas S. Wright	resid	fee	100	Slate river	10 SW	2.00		200.00	.20		1883 Thomas S. Wright of Campbell County, son of 1842 Thomas Wright of Buckingham County, grandson of 1813 John Wright of Buckingham County, and great grandson of 1809 John Wright of Buckingham County
Thomas Wright	resid	fee	881	On Same	10 SW	4.00	1500.00	3324.00	3.33		1842 Thomas Wright of Buckingham County, son of 1813 John Wright of Buckingham County and grandson of 1809 John Wright of Buckingham County
Helena Wright	resid	fee	100	Ws Wreck Island	29 W	7.00	100.00	700.00	.70	from Est Nathl. Hood	Helena (____) Wright, wife of 1881 William P. Wright of Appomattox County, a son of Charles Wright and grandson of Robert Wright, Sr. (Campbell County)

1841 LAND TAX LIST

BUCKINGHAM COUNTY, VIRGINIA

Appendix: Buckingham County, Virginia, 1841 Land Tax List:

Charles Patteson District No. 1:

Names of Owners	Residence	Kind of Estate	No. of Acres	Description or situation of the Land	Distance & bearing from the C House	Value of land pr acre including buildings	Sum added to the value of the Land on account of buildings	Total value of Land and buildings	Revenue	Remarks	Identification
William Wright	Resid	FS	145	Buffaloe Creek	14 E	3.00		435.00	.55		1863 William Wright of Buckingham County, probably son of 1803 John Wright of Cumberland County, grandson of 1770 John Wright of Cumberland County, and great grandson of 1769 George Wright of Essex County

Appendix: Buckingham County, Virginia, 1841 Land Tax List:

John T Bocock District No. 2:

Name of Owner	Residence	Kind of Estate	No. of Acres	description of Lands	Distance & bearing from the Court House	Value of Land or acre including buildings	Value of Buildings	Total Value Land & Buildings	Revenue Dols Cts		Identification
Thomas S Wright	resid	fee	100	Slate river	10 SW	2.00		200.00	.25		1883 Thomas S. Wright of Campbell County, son of 1842 Thomas Wright of Buckingham County, grandson of 1813 John Wright of Buckingham County, and great grandson of 1809 John Wright of Buckingham County
Thomas Wright	resid	fee	111	On Same	10 SW	9.00	900.00	799.00	2.25	375 to Tho. F Wright 395 to Anderson Wright	1842 Thomas Wright of Buckingham County, son of 1813 John Wright of Buckingham County and grandson of 1809 John Wright of Buckingham County
Thomas F Wright	resid	fee	375	On Middle Fork	10 W	3.25	300.00	1218.25	1.52	from Thomas Wright	1873 Thomas F. Wright of Buckingham County, probably son of 1842 Thomas Wright of Buckingham County, grandson of 1813 John Wright of Buckingham County, and great grandson of 1809 John Wright of Buckingham County

Appendix: Buckingham County, Virginia, 1841 Land Tax List:

John T Bocock District No. 2:

Name of Owner	Residence	Kind of Estate	No. of Acres	description of Lands	Distance & bearing from the Court House	Value of Land or acre including buildings	Value of Buildings	Total Value Land & Buildings	Revenue Dols Cts		Identification
Anderson Wright	resid	fee	395	Mill Cr & Middle Fork	11 W	3.20	300.00	1244.00	1.58	from Same	1891 James Anderson Wright, son of 1842 Thomas Wright of Buckingham County, grandson of 1813 John Wright of Buckingham County, and great grandson of 1809 John Wright of Buckingham County
Helena Wright	res	fee	100	Ws Wreck Island	29 W	7.00	100.00	700.00	.88		Helena (____) Wright, wife of 1881 William P. Wright of Appomattox County, a son of Charles Wright and grandson of Robert Wright, Sr. (Campbell County)

1842 LAND TAX LIST

BUCKINGHAM COUNTY, VIRGINIA

Appendix: Buckingham County, Virginia, 1842 Land Tax List:

District of Charles Patteson:

Names of Owners	Resi- dence	Kind of Estate	No. of Acres	Description or situation of the Land	Distance and bearing from the Courthouse	Value of Land including Buildings	Sum added to the Value of the Land on account of buildings	Totall Value of Land and buildings
William Wright	Res	FS	145	Buffaloe Cr	14 E	3.00		435.00

Appendix: Buckingham County, Virginia, 1842 Land Tax List:

Charles Patteson District No. 1:

Names of Owners [continued from prior page]	Revenue	Explanation of Alterations during the preceeding year especially from whom transferred	Identification
William Wright	.55		1863 William Wright of Buckingham County, probably son of 1803 John Wright of Cumberland County, grandson of 1770 John Wright of Cumberland County, and great grandson of 1769 George Wright of Essex County

Appendix: Buckingham County, Virginia, 1842 Land Tax List:

John T. Bocock District No. 2:

Names of Owners	Resi-dence	Kind of estate in fee or for life	No. of Acres	Description of the Tract of Land	Distance & Bearing from Court house	Value of the Land p Acre $ cts	Value of improve-ments $	Total Value of the tract of Land $ cts
Thomas S Wright			100	On Slate River	10 SW	2.00	200.00	
Thomas Wright Sen			111	On Same	10 W	9.00	900.00	999.00
Thomas F Wright			375	Adj Same		3.25	300.00	1318.75
Anderson Wright			395	Ad do		3.20	300.00	1264.00
Helena Wright			100	Ws Wreck Island	29 W	9.00	100.00	700.00
William Wright			115	Ws Slate River	11 W	1.00		115.00

Appendix: Buckingham County, Virginia, 1842 Land Tax List:

District of John T. Bocock:

Names of Owners [continued from prior page]	Tax Dollars Cents	Alterations & Remarks	Identification
Thomas S Wright	.25		1883 Thomas S. Wright of Campbell County, son of 1842 Thomas Wright of Buckingham County, grandson of 1813 John Wright of Buckingham County, and great grandson of 1809 John Wright of Buckingham County
Thomas Wright Sen	1.25		1842 Thomas Wright of Buckingham County, son of 1813 John Wright of Buckingham County and grandson of 1809 John Wright of Buckingham County
Thomas F Wright	1.52		1873 Thomas F. Wright of Buckingham County, probably son of 1842 Thomas Wright of Buckingham County, grandson of 1813 John Wright of Buckingham County, and great grandson of 1809 John Wright of Buckingham County
Anderson Wright	1.58		1891 James Anderson Wright, son of 1842 Thomas Wright of Buckingham County, grandson of 1813 John Wright of Buckingham County, and great grandson of 1809 John Wright of Buckingham County
Helena Wright	.88		Helena (____) Wright, wife of 1881 William P. Wright of Appomattox County, a son of Charles Wright and grandson of Robert Wright, Sr. (Campbell County)
William Wright	.15	from S P Hardwich & John R. Wigginson	1871 William R. Wright of Buckingham County, son of 1842 Thomas Wright of Buckingham County, grandson of 1813 John Wright of Buckingham County, and great grandson of 1809 John Wright of Buckingham County

1843 LAND TAX LIST

BUCKINGHAM COUNTY, VIRGINIA

Appendix: Buckingham County, Virginia, 1843 Land Tax List:

Charles Patteson District No. 1:

Name of Owner	Resi-dence	Estate whether held in Fee sim-ple or for life	No. of Acres	Description of land as to water courses mountains and con-tiguous tracts Distance and bear-ing from the C. House		Value of Land per acre including Buildings	Sum added to the land on act of buildings	Total Value of land & buildings	Amount of tax	Explanation of altera-tions during the preceed-ing year especially from whom transferred	Identification
William Wright	Res	F Simple	145	Buffaloe	14 E	3.00		435.00	.65		1863 William Wright of Buckingham County, probably son of 1803 John Wright of Cumberland County, grandson of 1770 John Wright of Cumberland County, and great grandson of 1769 George Wright of Essex County

Appendix: Buckingham County, Virginia, 1843 Land Tax List:

John T. Bocock District No. 2:

Names of Owners	Residence	Number Acres	Description	Distance & bearing from CH	Value of Land pr Acre		Total Value of the Land		last report	Identification
Thomas S Wright		100	On Same	10 SW	2.00		200.00	.30		1883 Thomas S. Wright of Campbell County, son of 1842 Thomas Wright of Buckingham County, grandson of 1813 John Wright of Buckingham County, and great grandson of 1809 John Wright of Buckingham County
Thomas Wright Senr		111	On Same	10 W	9.00	900.00	999.00	1.50		1842 Thomas Wright of Buckingham County, son of 1813 John Wright of Buckingham County and grandson of 1809 John Wright of Buckingham County
Thomas F Wright		375	Adj Same	10 W	3.25	300.00	1218.75	1.83		1873 Thomas F. Wright of Buckingham County, probably son of 1842 Thomas Wright of Buckingham County, grandson of 1813 John Wright of Buckingham County, and great grandson of 1809 John Wright of Buckingham County
Anderson Wright		395	Adj Same	10 W	3.20	300.00	1264.00	1.90		1891 James Anderson Wright, son of 1842 Thomas Wright of Buckingham County, grandson of 1813 John Wright of Buckingham County, and great grandson of 1809 John Wright of Buckingham County

Appendix: Buckingham County, Virginia, 1843 Land Tax List:

John T. Bocock District No. 2:

Names of Owners	Resi- dence		Number Acres	Description	Distance & bearing from CH	Value of Land pr Acre		Total Value of the Land		____ ____ ____ last report	Identification
Helena Wright			100	Ws Wr Isld	29 W	7.00	100.00	700.00	1.05		Helena (____) Wright, wife of 1881 William P. Wright of Appomattox County, a son of Charles Wright and grandson of Robert Wright, Sr. (Campbell County)
William Wright			115	Ws Slate River	11 W	1.00		115.00	.17		1871 William R. Wright of Buckingham County, son of 1842 Thomas Wright of Buckingham County, grandson of 1813 John Wright of Buckingham County, and great grandson of 1809 John Wright of Buckingham County
Thomas P. Wright S Davd	Res		250	W Slate River	13 W	3.00	100.00	750.00	1.13	from Henry Bagby's heirs	1880 Thomas P. Wright of Buckingham County, son of David M. Wright, Sr. (Buckingham County)

1844 LAND TAX LIST

BUCKINGHAM COUNTY, VIRGINIA

Appendix: Buckingham County, Virginia, 1844 Land Tax List:

Charles Patteson District No. 1:

Name of Owner	Resi-dence	Estate whether held in fee sim-ple for life &c	No Acres	Description of the land as to water courses contiguous tracts &c	Distance and bearing from the C House	Value of land pr acre Including Buildings	Sum added to the land on act of Buildings	Total Value of land & buildings	Amt. of tax on the whole tract at the legal rate	Explanation of altera-tions during the preceed-ing year especially from whom transferred	Identification
William Wright	Res	F Simp	145	Buffaloe Creek	14 E	3.00		435.00	.55		1863 William Wright of Buckingham County, probably son of 1803 John Wright of Cumberland County, grandson of 1770 John Wright of Cumberland County, and great grandson of 1769 George Wright of Essex County

Appendix: Buckingham County, Virginia, 1844 Land Tax List:

John T. Bocock District No. 2:

Name of the Owner	Resi- dence	Kind of Estate	Number of Acres	Description of the tract of land	Distance & Bearing from CH	Value of Land pr Acre Dol cts	Value of Build- ings Dol.	Total Value of the Tract Dol Cts	Revenue Dol. Cts	Alterations since the last report	Identification
Thomas S Wright			100	Ws Same	10 SW	2.00		200.00	.25		1883 Thomas S. Wright of Campbell County, son of 1842 Thomas Wright of Buckingham County, grandson of 1813 John Wright of Buckingham County, and great grandson of 1809 John Wright of Buckingham County
Thomas Wright Senr			111	On Same	10 W	9.00	900.00	999.00	1.25		1842 Thomas Wright of Buckingham County, son of 1813 John Wright of Buckingham County and grandson of 1809 John Wright of Buckingham County
Thomas F Wright			325	Adj Same	10 W	3.25	300.00	1056.25	1.32	50 to Richd Robertson	1873 Thomas F. Wright of Buckingham County, probably son of 1842 Thomas Wright of Buckingham County, grandson of 1813 John Wright of Buckingham County, and great grandson of 1809 John Wright of Buckingham County

Appendix: Buckingham County, Virginia, 1844 Land Tax List:

John T. Bocock District No. 2:

Name of the Owner	Resi- dence	Kind of Estate	Number of Acres	Description of the tract of land	Distance & Bearing from CH	Value of Land pr Acre Dol cts	Value of Build- ings Dol.	Total Value of the Tract Dol Cts	Revenue Dol. Cts	Alterations since the last report	Identification
Anderson Wright			395	Adj Same	10 W	3.20	300.00	1264.00	1.58		1891 James Anderson Wright, son of 1842 Thomas Wright of Buckingham County, grandson of 1813 John Wright of Buckingham County, and great grandson of 1809 John Wright of Buckingham County
Helena Wright			100	Ws Wreck Island	29 W	7.00	100.00	700.00	.88		Helena (____) Wright, wife of 1881 William P. Wright of Appomattox County, a son of Charles Wright and grandson of Robert Wright, Sr. (Campbell County)
William Wright			115	Ws Slate River	11 W	1.00		115.00	.15		1871 William R. Wright of Buckingham County, son of 1842 Thomas Wright of Buckingham County, grandson of 1813 John Wright of Buckingham County, and great grandson of 1809 John Wright of Buckingham County
Tho. P. Wright S David	Resid		250	Ws Slate River	13 W	3.00	100.00	750.00	.94		1880 Thomas P. Wright of Buckingham County, son of David M. Wright, Sr. (Buckingham County)

1845 LAND TAX LIST

BUCKINGHAM COUNTY, VIRGINIA

Residence	...d in fee simple, for life, &c	No. of Acres	...iption the land as to water-courses, mountains and contiguous tracts &c	Distance and bearing from the court-house	Value of land per acre, including buildings	Sum added to the land on account of buildings	Total value of the land and buildings	Amt. of tax on the whole tract, at the legal rate	Explanation of alterations during the preceding year especially from whom transferred	Identification
W...am Wright	Resdt	F Simp	145	On Buffaloe	14 E	3.00		435.00	.44		1863 William Wright of Buckingham County, probably son of 1803 John Wright of Cumberland County, grandson of 1770 John Wright of Cumberland County, and great grandson of 1769 George Wright of Essex County

Appendix: Buckingham County, Virginia, 1845 Land Tax List:

Granderson Moseley District No. 2:

Name of Owner	Resi-dence	Estate whether held in fee sim-ple, for life, &c	No. of Acres	Description of the land as to water-courses, mountains and conti-guous tracts &c	Distance and bear-ing from the court-house	Value of land per acre, including buildings	Sum added to the land on account of buildings	Total value of the land and buildings	Amt. of tax on the whole tract, at the legal rate	Explanation of altera-tions during the preced-ing year especially from whom transferred	Identification
Thomas S Wright	Buckhm	Fee	100	Ws Slate River	10 SW	2.00		200.00	.20		1883 Thomas S. Wright of Campbell County, son of 1842 Thomas Wright of Buckingham County, grandson of 1813 John Wright of Buckingham County, and great grandson of 1809 John Wright of Buckingham County
Thomas Wright Sr Est	Buckhm	Fee	111	Ws Slate River	10 W	9.00	800.00	999.00	1.00		Estate of 1842 Thomas Wright of Buckingham County, son of 1813 John Wright of Buckingham County and grandson of 1809 John Wright of Buckingham County
Thomas F Wright	Buckhm	Fee	325	Adj Ws Slate River	10 W	3.25	300.00	1056.25	1.66		1873 Thomas F. Wright of Buckingham County, probably son of 1842 Thomas Wright of Buckingham County, grandson of 1813 John Wright of Buckingham County, and great grandson of 1809 John Wright of Buckingham County

Appendix: Buckingham County, Virginia, 1845 Land Tax List:

Granderson Moseley District No. 2:

Name of Owner	Resi-dence	Estate whether held in fee sim-ple, for life, &c	No. of Acres	Description of the land as to water-courses, mountains and conti-guous tracts &c	Distance and bear-ing from the court-house	Value of land per acre, including buildings	Sum added to the land on account of buildings	Total value of the land and buildings	Amt. of tax on the whole tract, at the legal rate	Explanation of altera-tions during the preced-ing year especially from whom transferred	Identification
James A Wright	Buckhm	Fee	395	Ws Slate River	10 W	3.20	300.00	1264.00	1.27		1891 James Anderson Wright, son of 1842 Thomas Wright of Buckingham County, grandson of 1813 John Wright of Buckingham County, and great grandson of 1809 John Wright of Buckingham County
William Wright	Buckhm	Fee	115	Ws Slate river	11 W	1.00		115.00	.12		1871 William R. Wright of Buckingham County, son of 1842 Thomas Wright of Buckingham County, grandson of 1813 John Wright of Buckingham County, and great grandson of 1809 John Wright of Buckingham County
Thomas P Wright	Buckhm	Fee	250	Bagby's	13 W	5.00	100.00	750.00	.75		1880 Thomas P. Wright of Buckingham County, son of David M. Wright, Sr. (Buckingham County)

1846 LAND TAX LIST

BUCKINGHAM COUNTY, VIRGINIA

Appendix: Buckingham County, Virginia, 1846 Land Tax List:

Charles Patteson District No. 1:

Name of Owner	Resi-dence	Estate whether held in fee sim-ple, for life, &c	No. of Acres	Description of the land as to water-courses, mountains and conti-guous tracts &c	Distance and bear-ing from the court-house	Value of land per acre, including buildings	Sum added to the land on account of buildings	Total value of the land and buildings	Amt. of tax on the whole tract, at the legal rate	Explanation of altera-tions during the preced-ing year especially from whom transferred	Identification
William Wright	Res	F Simp	145	On Buffaloe Creek	14 E	3.00		435.00	.44		1863 William Wright of Buckingham County, probably son of 1803 John Wright of Cumberland County, grandson of 1770 John Wright of Cumberland County, and great grandson of 1769 George Wright of Essex County

Appendix: Buckingham County, Virginia, 1846 Land Tax List:

Granderson Moseley District No. 2:

Name of Owner	Resi-dence	Estate whether held in fee sim-ple, for life, &c	No. of Acres	Description of the land as to water-courses, mountains and conti-guous tracts &c	Distance and bear-ing from the court-house	Value of land per acre, including buildings	Sum added to the land on account of buildings	Total value of the land and buildings	Amt. of tax on the whole tract, at the legal rate	Explanation of altera-tions during the preced-ing year especially from whom transferred	Identification
Thomas S Wright	Res	Fee	100	Ws S. R	10 SW	2.00		200.00	.20		1883 Thomas S. Wright of Campbell County, son of 1842 Thomas Wright of Buckingham County, grandson of 1813 John Wright of Buckingham County, and great grandson of 1809 John Wright of Buckingham County
Thomas Wright Est	Res	Fee	111	Ws S. R	10 SW	9.00	800.00	999.00	1.00		Estate of 1842 Thomas Wright of Buckingham County, son of 1813 John Wright of Buckingham County and grandson of 1809 John Wright of Buckingham County
Thomas F Wright	Res	Fee	325	Ws S. R	10 SW	3.25	300.00	1056.25	1.66		1873 Thomas F. Wright of Buckingham County, probably son of 1842 Thomas Wright of Buckingham County, grandson of 1813 John Wright of Buckingham County, and great grandson of 1809 John Wright of Buckingham County

Appendix: Buckingham County, Virginia, 1846 Land Tax List:

Granderson Moseley District No. 2:

Name of Owner	Resi-dence	Estate whether held in fee sim-ple, for life, &c	No. of Acres	Description of the land as to water-courses, mountains and conti-guous tracts &c	Distance and bear-ing from the court-house	Value of land per acre, including buildings	Sum added to the land on account of buildings	Total value of the land and buildings	Amt. of tax on the whole tract, at the legal rate	Explanation of altera-tions during the preced-ing year especially from whom transferred	Identification
James A Wright	Res	Fee	395	Ws S. R	10 SW	3.20	300.00	1264.00	1.27		1891 James Anderson Wright, son of 1842 Thomas Wright of Buckingham County, grandson of 1813 John Wright of Buckingham County, and great grandson of 1809 John Wright of Buckingham County
William Wright	Res	Fee	115	Ws S R	12 W	1.00		115.00	.12		1871 William R. Wright of Buckingham County, son of 1842 Thomas Wright of Buckingham County, grandson of 1813 John Wright of Buckingham County, and great grandson of 1809 John Wright of Buckingham County
Thomas P Wright	Res	Fee	250	Bagbys	13 W	3.00	100.00	750.00	.75		1880 Thomas P. Wright of Buckingham County, son of David M. Wright, Sr. (Buckingham County)

1847 LAND TAX LIST

BUCKINGHAM COUNTY, VIRGINIA

Appendix: Buckingham County, Virginia, 1847 Land Tax List:

John A. Lancaster District No. 1:

Name of Owner	Residence	Estate whether held in fee simple, for life, &c	No. of Acres	Description of the land as to watercourses, mountains and contiguous tracts &c	Distance and bearing from the courthouse	Value of land per acre, including buildings	Sum added to the land on account of buildings	Total value of the land and buildings	Amt. of tax on the whole tract, at the legal rate	Explanation of alterations during the preceding year especially from whom transferred	Identification
William Wright	Res	F S	145	On Buffaloe Cr	_ E	3.00		435.00	.44		1863 William Wright of Buckingham County, probably son of 1803 John Wright of Cumberland County, grandson of 1770 John Wright of Cumberland County, and great grandson of 1769 George Wright of Essex County

Appendix: Buckingham County, Virginia, 1847 Land Tax List:

Granderson Moseley District No. 2:

Name of Owner	Resi-dence	Estate whether held in fee sim-ple, for life, &c	No. of Acres	Description of the land as to water-courses, mountains and conti-guous tracts &c	Distance and bear-ing from the court-house	Value of land per acre, including buildings	Sum added to the land on account of buildings	Total value of the land and buildings	Amt. of tax on the whole tract, at the legal rate	Explanation of altera-tions during the preced-ing year especially from whom transferred	Identification
Thos S Wright	Res	Fee	100	Ws S R	10 SW	2.00		200.00	.20		1883 Thomas S. Wright of Campbell County, son of 1842 Thomas Wright of Buckingham County, grandson of 1813 John Wright of Buckingham County, and great grandson of 1809 John Wright of Buckingham County
Thomas Wright Est	Res	Fee	111	Ws S R	10 SW	9.00	800.00	999.00	1.00		Estate of 1842 Thomas Wright of Buckingham County, son of 1813 John Wright of Buckingham County and grandson of 1809 John Wright of Buckingham County
Thomas F Wright	Res	Fee	325	Ws S R	10 SW	3.25	300.00	1056.25	1.06		1873 Thomas F. Wright of Buckingham County, probably son of 1842 Thomas Wright of Buckingham County, grandson of 1813 John Wright of Buckingham County, and great grandson of 1809 John Wright of Buckingham County

Appendix: Buckingham County, Virginia, 1847 Land Tax List:

Granderson Moseley District No. 2:

Name of Owner	Residence	Estate whether held in fee simple, for life, &c	No. of Acres	Description of the land as to watercourses, mountains and contiguous tracts &c	Distance and bearing from the courthouse	Value of land per acre, including buildings	Sum added to the land on account of buildings	Total value of the land and buildings	Amt. of tax on the whole tract, at the legal rate	Explanation of alterations during the preceding year especially from whom transferred	Identification
James A Wright	Res	Fee	395	Ws S R	10 SW	3.20	300.00	1264.00	1.27		1891 James Anderson Wright, son of 1842 Thomas Wright of Buckingham County, grandson of 1813 John Wright of Buckingham County, and great grandson of 1809 John Wright of Buckingham County
William R Wright	Res	Fee	115	Ws S R	10 SW	1.00		115.00	.12		1871 William R. Wright of Buckingham County, son of 1842 Thomas Wright of Buckingham County, grandson of 1813 John Wright of Buckingham County, and great grandson of 1809 John Wright of Buckingham County
Thomas P Wright	Res	Fee	250	Bagbys	13 W	3.00	100.00	750.00	.75		1880 Thomas P. Wright of Buckingham County, son of David M. Wright, Sr. (Buckingham County)

1848 LAND TAX LIST

BUCKINGHAM COUNTY, VIRGINIA

Appendix: Buckingham County, Virginia, 1848 Land Tax List:

William P. Kyle District No. 1:

Name of Owner	Resi-dence	Estate whether held in fee sim-ple, for life, &c	No. of Acres	Description of the land as to water-courses, mountains and conti-guous tracts &c	Distance and bear-ing from the court-house	Value of land per acre, including buildings	Sum added to the land on account of buildings	Total value of the land and buildings	Amt. of tax on the whole tract, at the legal rate	Explanation of altera-tions during the preced-ing year especially from whom transferred	Identification
William Wright	Res	F S	145	On Buffalo	14 E	3.00		435.00	.44		1863 William Wright of Buckingham County, probably son of 1803 John Wright of Cumberland County, grandson of 1770 John Wright of Cumberland County, and great grandson of 1769 George Wright of Essex County

Appendix: Buckingham County, Virginia, 1848 Land Tax List:

Granderson Moseley District No. 2:

Name of Owner	Resi-dence	Estate whether held in fee sim-ple, for life, &c	No. of Acres	Description of the land as to water-courses, mountains and conti-guous tracts &c	Distance and bear-ing from the court-house	Value of land per acre, including buildings	Sum added to the land on account of buildings	Total value of the land and buildings	Amt. of tax on the whole tract, at the legal rate	Explanation of altera-tions during the preced-ing year especially from whom transferred	Identification
Thos S Wright	Apptx	Fee	100	Ws S R	10 SW	2.00		200.00	.20		1883 Thomas S. Wright of Campbell County, son of 1842 Thomas Wright of Buckingham County, grandson of 1813 John Wright of Buckingham County, and great grandson of 1809 John Wright of Buckingham County
Thomas Wright Est	Res	Fee	111	Ws S R	10 SW	9.00	800.00	999.00	1.00		Estate of 1842 Thomas Wright of Buckingham County, son of 1813 John Wright of Buckingham County and grandson of 1809 John Wright of Buckingham County
Thomas F Wright	Res	Fee	325	Ws S R	10 SW	3.25	300.00	1056.25	1.06		1873 Thomas F. Wright of Buckingham County, probably son of 1842 Thomas Wright of Buckingham County, grandson of 1813 John Wright of Buckingham County, and great grandson of 1809 John Wright of Buckingham County

Appendix: Buckingham County, Virginia, 1848 Land Tax List:

Granderson Moseley District No. 2:

Name of Owner	Resi-dence	Estate whether held in fee sim-ple, for life, &c	No. of Acres	Description of the land as to water-courses, mountains and conti-guous tracts &c	Distance and bear-ing from the court-house	Value of land per acre, including buildings	Sum added to the land on account of buildings	Total value of the land and buildings	Amt. of tax on the whole tract, at the legal rate	Explanation of altera-tions during the preced-ing year especially from whom transferred	Identification
James A Wright	Res	Fee	395	Ws S R	10 SW	3.20	300.00	1264.00	1.27		1891 James Anderson Wright, son of 1842 Thomas Wright of Buckingham County, grandson of 1813 John Wright of Buckingham County, and great grandson of 1809 John Wright of Buckingham County
Wm R Wright	Res	Fee	115	Ws S R	10 SW	1.00	100.00	230.00	.23	Impts added	1871 William R. Wright of Buckingham County, son of 1842 Thomas Wright of Buckingham County, grandson of 1813 John Wright of Buckingham County, and great grandson of 1809 John Wright of Buckingham County
Thomas P Wright	Res	Fee	250	Bagbys	13 W	3.00	100.00	750.00	.75		1880 Thomas P. Wright of Buckingham County, son of David M. Wright, Sr. (Buckingham County)

1849 LAND TAX LIST

BUCKINGHAM COUNTY, VIRGINIA

Appendix: Buckingham County, Virginia, 1849 Land Tax List:

William P. Kyle District No. 1:

Name of Owner	Residence	Estate whether held in fee simple, for life, &c	No. of Acres	Description of the land as to watercourses, mountains and contiguous tracts &c	Distance and bearing from the courthouse	Value of land per acre, including buildings	Sum added to the land on account of buildings	Total value of the land and buildings	Amt. of tax on the whole tract, at the legal rate	Explanation of alterations during the preceding year especially from whom transferred	Identification
William Wright	R	F S	145	On Buffalo do	14 E	3.00		435.00	.44		1863 William Wright of Buckingham County, probably son of 1803 John Wright of Cumberland County, grandson of 1770 John Wright of Cumberland County, and great grandson of 1769 George Wright of Essex County

Appendix: Buckingham County, Virginia, 1849 Land Tax List:

Granderson Moseley District No. 2:

Name of Owner	Residence	Estate whether held in fee simple, for life, &c	No. of Acres	Description of the land as to watercourses, mountains and contiguous tracts &c	Distance and bearing from the courthouse	Value of land per acre, including buildings	Sum added to the land on account of buildings	Total value of the land and buildings	Amt. of tax on the whole tract, at the legal rate	Explanation of alterations during the preceding year especially from whom transferred	Identification
Thomas S Wright	Apptx	Fee	100	Ws S R	10 SW	2.00		200.00	.20		1883 Thomas S. Wright of Campbell County, son of 1842 Thomas Wright of Buckingham County, grandson of 1813 John Wright of Buckingham County, and great grandson of 1809 John Wright of Buckingham County
Thomas Wright Est	Res	Fee	111	Ws S R	10 SW	9.00	800.00	999.00	1.00		Estate of 1842 Thomas Wright of Buckingham County, son of 1813 John Wright of Buckingham County and grandson of 1809 John Wright of Buckingham County
Thomas F Wright	Res	Fee	325	Ws S R	10 SW	3.25	300.00	1056.25	1.06		1873 Thomas F. Wright of Buckingham County, probably son of 1842 Thomas Wright of Buckingham County, grandson of 1813 John Wright of Buckingham County, and great grandson of 1809 John Wright of Buckingham County

Appendix: Buckingham County, Virginia, 1849 Land Tax List:

Granderson Moseley District No. 2:

Name of Owner	Residence	Estate whether held in fee simple, for life, &c	No. of Acres	Description of the land as to watercourses, mountains and contiguous tracts &c	Distance and bearing from the courthouse	Value of land per acre, including buildings	Sum added to the land on account of buildings	Total value of the land and buildings	Amt. of tax on the whole tract, at the legal rate	Explanation of alterations during the preceding year especially from whom transferred	Identification
James A Wright	Res	Fee	395	Ws S R	10 SW	3.20	300.00	1264.00	1.27		1891 James Anderson Wright, son of 1842 Thomas Wright of Buckingham County, grandson of 1813 John Wright of Buckingham County, and great grandson of 1809 John Wright of Buckingham County
William R Wright	Res	Fee	115	Ws S R	10 SW	1.00	100.00	230.00	.23		1871 William R. Wright of Buckingham County, son of 1842 Thomas Wright of Buckingham County, grandson of 1813 John Wright of Buckingham County, and great grandson of 1809 John Wright of Buckingham County
Thomas P Wright	Res	Fee	250	Bagbys	13 W	3.00	100.00	750.00	.75		1880 Thomas P. Wright of Buckingham County, son of David M. Wright, Sr. (Buckingham County)

1850 LAND TAX LIST

BUCKINGHAM COUNTY, VIRGINIA

Appendix: Buckingham County, Virginia, 1850 Land Tax List:

William P. Kyle District No. 1:

Name of Owner	Residence	Estate whether held in fee simple, for life, &c	No. of Acres	Description of the land as to watercourses, mountains and contiguous tracts &c	Distance and bearing from the courthouse	Value of land per acre, including buildings	Sum added to the land on account of buildings	Total value of the land and buildings	Amt. of tax on the whole tract, at the legal rate	Explanation of alterations during the preceding year especially from whom transferred	Identification
William Wright	Res	F S	145	On Buffalo	14 E	3.00		435.00	.44		1863 William Wright of Buckingham Creek County, probably son of 1803 John Wright of Cumberland County, grandson of 1770 John Wright of Cumberland County, and great grandson of 1769 George Wright of Essex County

Appendix: Buckingham County, Virginia, 1850 Land Tax List:

Granderson Moseley District No. 2:

Name of Owner	Resi-dence	Estate whether held in fee sim-ple, for life, &c	No. of Acres	Description of the land as to water-courses, mountains and conti-guous tracts &c	Distance and bear-ing from the court-house	Value of land per acre, including buildings	Sum added to the land on account of buildings	Total value of the land and buildings	Amt. of tax on the whole tract, at the legal rate	Explanation of altera-tions during the preced-ing year especially from whom transferred	Identification
Thos S Wright	Apptx	Fee	100	Ws S R	10 W	2.00		200.00	.20		1883 Thomas S. Wright of Campbell County, son of 1842 Thomas Wright of Buckingham County, grandson of 1813 John Wright of Buckingham County, and great grandson of 1809 John Wright of Buckingham County
Thos Wright Est	Res	Fee	111	Ws S R	10 W	9.00	800.00	999.00	1.00		Estate of 1842 Thomas Wright of Buckingham County, son of 1813 John Wright of Buckingham County and grandson of 1809 John Wright of Buckingham County
James A Wright	Res	Fee	395	Ws S R	10 W	3.20	300.00	1264.00	1.27		1891 James Anderson Wright, son of 1842 Thomas Wright of Buckingham County, grandson of 1813 John Wright of Buckingham County, and great grandson of 1809 John Wright of Buckingham County

Appendix: Buckingham County, Virginia, 1850 Land Tax List:

Granderson Moseley District No. 2:

Name of Owner	Resi-dence	Estate whether held in fee sim-ple, for life, &c	No. of Acres	Description of the land as to water-courses, mountains and conti-guous tracts &c	Distance and bear-ing from the court-house	Value of land per acre, including buildings	Sum added to the land on account of buildings	Total value of the land and buildings	Amt. of tax on the whole tract, at the legal rate	Explanation of altera-tions during the preced-ing year especially from whom transferred	Identification
Thos F Wright	Res	Fee	325	Ws S R	10 W	3.25	300.00	1056.25	1.06		1873 Thomas F. Wright of Buckingham County, probably son of 1842 Thomas Wright of Buckingham County, grandson of 1813 John Wright of Buckingham County, and great grandson of 1809 John Wright of Buckingham County
Wm R Wright	Res	Fee	115	Ws S R	10 W	2.00	100.00	230.00	.23		1871 William R. Wright of Buckingham County, son of 1842 Thomas Wright of Buckingham County, grandson of 1813 John Wright of Buckingham County, and great grandson of 1809 John Wright of Buckingham County
Thomas P Wright	Res	Fee	250	Bagbys	13 W	3.00	100.00	750.00	.75		1880 Thomas P. Wright of Buckingham County, son of David M. Wright, Sr. (Buckingham County)

WRIGHT FAMILY

DEATH RECORDS

1856 TO 1920

BUCKINGHAM COUNTY, VIRGINIA

Revised as of June 30, 2025

Introduction To Appendix: Death Records, Buckingham County, Virginia

This document is an appendix to a larger work titled *Sorting Some Of The Wrights Of Southern Virginia*. The work is divided into parts for each family of Wrights that has been researched. Each part is divided into two sections; the first section is text discussing the family and the evidence supporting the relationships and the second section is a descendants chart summarizing the relationships and information known about each individual.

The appendices to the work (of which this document is one) present source records for persons named Wright by county and by type of record with the identification of the person named and their Wright ancestors to the extent known.

The source for the records listed in this appendix is the following:

1) Buckingham County, Virginia, Death Records available from the Commonwealth of Virginia, Department of Health, Division of Vital Records, P.O. Box 1000, Richmond, Virginia 23208-1000.

2) Buckingham County, Virginia, Death Records 1853-1868, by Jeanne Stinson, Iberian Publishing Company, Athens, Georgia, 2000.

The identification of a person or their ancestor by year and county indicates their year of death and county of residence at death. For example, "1763 Thomas Wright of Bedford County" indicates that this was the Thomas Wright who died in 1763 in Bedford County. If no state is listed after the county, the state is Virginia; counties in states other than Virginia will have a state listed after the county, as in "1876 William S. Wright of Highland County, Ohio".

A parenthetical after the name indicates an identification of the person when a place of death is not yet known, as in "John Wright (Goochland County Carpenter)". A county in parentheses after the name indicates the county with which that person was most identified when no evidence of the place of death has yet been found, as in "Grief Wright (Bedford County)".

All or portions of the text and descendants charts for each Wright family identified are available from the author:

Robert N. Grant
15 Campo Bello Court
Menlo Park, California 94025

(H) 650-854-0895
RNGrant@grantandgordon.com

This is a work in process and I would be most interested in receiving additional information about any of the persons identified in these records in order to correct any errors or expand on the information given.

Book/Page	Date	Decedent	Information	Identification
Reg 109	1853/12/00	Addison Wright	Place: Buckingham County, Virginia Race: White Sex:: Male Place: Buckingham Cause: Typhoid Fever Parents Names: _____ & Caty Wright Informant: E. W. Cabell	
038 084	1854/04/05	Alfred _____	Place: Buckingham County, Virginia Race: Sex:: Male Owner: William Wright Cause: lungs Parents Names: Informant: Owner	
043 079	1856/02/25	Daid _____	Place: Buckingham County, Virginia Race: Sex: Male Age: 6 months Owner: Thomas F. Wright Cause: Parents Names: Informant: Owner	
049 016	1858/05/10	Randolph _____	Place: Buckingham County, Virginia Race: Sex: Male Age: 65 Owner: Thomas P. Wright Place: Buckingham Cause: Gravel Informant: Owner	

Appendix: Buckingham County, Virginia Index of Death Records

Book/Page	Date	Decedent	Information	Identification
Reg 085	1858/00/00	Jane Wright	Place: Buckingham County, Virginia Race: White Sex: Female	Jane R. (_____) Wright, wife of 1863 William Wright of Buckingham County, a son of 1803 John Wright of Buckingham County, grandson of 1770 John Wright of Cumberland County, and great grandson of 1769 George Wright of Essex County
Reg 137	1861/02/10	John Wright	Place: Buckingham County, Virginia Race: White Sex: Male Age: 4 days Place: Buckingham Parents Names: Jas. A. & Elizth. Wright Informant: Wm. Wright Relation of Informant: Grandfather	1861 John Wright of Buckingham County, son of 1905 James A. Wright of Buckingham County, grandson of 1863 William Wright of Buckingham County, great grandson of 1803 John Wright of Cumberland County, great great grandson of 1770 John Wright of Cumberland County, and great great great grandson of 1769 George Wright of Essex County
Reg 030	1861/12/11	Mary F. Wright	Place: Buckingham County, Virginia Race: White Sex: Female Age: 29 Cause: Child Bed Consort of: Jas. A. Wright Informant: Jas A. Wright Relation of Informant: Husband	Mary F. (McCraw) Wright, wife of 1891 James Anderson Wright of Buckingham County, a son of 1842 Thomas Wright of Buckingham County, grandson of 1813 John Wright of Buckingham County, and great grandson of 1809 John Wright of Buckingham County
Reg 111	1862/04/07	Jordon Wright	Place: Buckingham County, Virginia Race: White Sex: Male Age: 19 Cause: Measles Parents Names: Thos. & Lucy Wright Consort of: Unmarried Informant: Thos. P. Wright Relation of Informant: Father	1862 Jordan Wright of Buckingham County, son of 1880 Thomas P. Wright of Buckingham County and grandson of 1840 David M. Wright, Sr., (Buckingham County)

Appendix: Buckingham County, Virginia Index of Death Records

Book/Page	Date	Decedent	Information	Identification
074 019	1862/12/13	Lonze ____	Place: Buckingham County, Virginia Race: Sex: Male Age: 5 months Owner: William Wright Cause: Croup Informant: Owner	
074 020	1862/01/14	Jim ____	Place: Buckingham County, Virginia Race: Sex: Male Age: 8 months Owner: William Wright Cause: Cold Informant: Owner	
Reg 016	1866/04/00	James Wright	Place: Buckingham County, Virginia Race: Colored Sex: Female Age: 1 Parents Names: Geo. & Martha Wright Birthplace: Buckingham Informant: G. & M. Wright Relation of Informant: Parents	1866 James Wright of Buckingham County, son of George Wright
Reg 017	1866/04/00	____ Wright	Place: Buckingham County, Virginia Race: Colored Sex: Female Age: 1 Parents Names: Wm. & Mag Wright Birthplace: Buckingham Informant: W. & M. Wright Relation of Informant: Parents	

Appendix: Buckingham County, Virginia Index of Death Records

Book/Page	Date	Decedent	Information	Identification
Reg 025	1867/07/00	Mary A. Wright	Place: Buckingham County, Virginia Race: Colored Sex: Female Age: 20 Place: Buckingham Cause: Childbirth Parents Names: _____ & May Wright Birthplace: Buckingham Informant: Jim Wright Relation of Informant: Father	
099 011	1867/11/00	_____ Wright	Place: Buckingham County, Virginia Race: Black Sex: Male Parents: Jim & May Wright Place: Buckingham Cause: Informant: Father	
Reg 036	1871/10/00	William R. Wright	Place: Buckingham County or Appomattox County, Virginia Race: White Sex: Male Age: 63 Cause: Apoplexy Parents Names: Thomas & _____ Birthplace: Buckingham Occupation: Farmer Consort of: Lavina Wright Informant: L. Wright Relation of Informant: Widow	1871 William R. Wright of Buckingham County, son of 1842 Thomas Wright of Buckingham County, grandson of 1813 John Wright of Buckingham County, and great grandson of 1809 John Wright of Buckingham County

Book/Page	Date	Decedent	Information	Identification
Reg 029	1872/02/00	Branch B. Wright	Place: Buckingham County, Virginia Race: White Sex: Male Age: 4 Cause: Brain Fever Parents Names: Wm. W. & Susan Birthplace: Buckingham Informant: Wm. W. Wright Relation of Informant: Father	1872 Branch B. Wright of Buckingham County, son of 1893 William Wesley Wright of Appomattox County
Reg 030	1872/04/01	Amanda Wright	Place: Buckingham County, Virginia Race: White Sex: Female Age: 3 Cause: Worms Parents Names: Wm. W. & Susan Birthplace: Buckingham Informant: Wm. W. Wright Relation of Informant: Father	Amanda Wright, daughter of 1893 William Wesley Wright of Appomattox County
Reg 025	1873/07/00	C. G. Wright	Place: Buckingham County, Virginia Race: White Sex: Female Age: 1 year & 10 months Cause: Whooping Parents Names: Jas. L. & Pattie L. Wright Birthplace: Buckingham Informant: Jas. L. Wright Relation of Informant: Father	

Appendix: Buckingham County, Virginia Index of Death Records

Book/Page	Date	Decedent	Information	Identification
Reg 010	1873/03/17	Thos. F. Wright	Place: Buckingham County, Virginia Race: White Sex: Male Age: 49 Cause: Apoplexy Parents Names: Thos. Wright & _____ Occupation: Farmer Consort of: Unmarried Informant: T. Wright	1873 Thomas F. Wright of Buckingham County, probably son of 1842 Thomas Wright of Buckingham County, grandson of 1813 John Wright of Buckingham County, and great grandson of 1809 John Wright of Buckingham County
059	1877/12/18	Pattie Wright	Place: Buckingham County, Virginia Race: Colored Sex: Female Age: 23 Cause: Consumption Birthplace: Buckingham Consort of: Willis Wright Informant: Willis Wright Relation of Informant: Husband	Pattie (Jones) Wright, wife of Willis Wright, a son of 1892 Dick Wright of Buckingham County
096	1880/09/25	Thomas P. Wright	Place: Buckingham County, Virginia Race: White Sex: Male Age: 75 Cause: Heart Disease Birthplace: Buckingham Informant: Lucy Wright Relation of Informant: Wife	1880 Thomas P. Wright of Buckingham County, son of 1840 David M. Wright, Sr. (Buckingham County)

Appendix: Buckingham County, Virginia Index of Death Records

Book/Page	Date	Decedent	Information	Identification
078	1882/01/12	William H. Wright	Place: Buckingham County, Virginia Race: White Sex: Male Age: 39 Cause: Pneumonia Birthplace: Buckingham Consort of: Married Informant: Mrs. W. H. Wright Relation of Informant: Wife	1882 William H. Wright of Buckingham County, son of 1871 William R. Wright of Buckingham County, grandson of 1842 Thomas Wright of Buckingham County, great grandson of 1813 John Wright of Buckingham County, and great great grandson of 1809 John Wright of Buckingham County
070	1882/05/18	Bessie Wright	Place: Buckingham County, Virginia Race: White Sex: Female Age: 4 months Cause: Whooping Cough Parents Names: Thos. J. & Bettie H. Wright Birthplace: Buckingham County, Virginia Consort of: Unmarried Informant: Tho. J. Wright Relation of Informant: Father	Bessie Wright, daughter of Thomas J. Wright, granddaughter of 1871 William R. Wright of Buckingham County, great granddaughter of 1842 Thomas Wright of Buckingham County, great great granddaughter of 1813 John Wright of Buckingham County, and great great great granddaughter of 1809 John Wright of Buckingham County
053	1883/02/09	Sue Wright	Place: Buckingham County, Virginia Race: White Sex: Female Age: 67 Cause: Paralysis Parents Names: Charles & Charlott Wright Birthplace: Buckingham Consort of: Married Informant: Willie Wright Relation of Informant: Husband	

Appendix: Buckingham County, Virginia Index of Death Records

Book/Page	Date	Decedent	Information	Identification
055	1884/04/03	Mary Wright	Place: Buckingham County, Virginia Race: Colored Sex: Female Age: 33 Parents Names: Sue & Tom Wright Birthplace: Buckingham Occupation: Farmer Consort of: Married Informant: Tom Wright Relation of Informant: Father	
075	1884/07/00	Geo. W. Wright	Place: Buckingham County, Virginia Race: White Sex: Male Age: 29 Cause: Killed by fall Parents Names: Jas. & Elizabeth Wright Birthplace: Buckingham Occupation: Farmer Informant: James Wright Relation of Informant: Father	1884 George W. Wright of Buckingham County, son of 1905 James A. Wright of Buckingham County, grandson of 1863 William Wright of Buckingham County, great grandson of 1803 John Wright of Cumberland County, great great grandson of 1770 John Wright of Cumberland County, and great great great grandson of 1769 George Wright of Essex County
058	1884/08/04	Nannie Wright	Place: Buckingham County, Virginia Race: White Sex: Female Age: 1 year & 6 months Parents Names: L. W. & Rachel Wright Birthplace: Buckingham Consort of: Single Informant: L. W. Wright Relation of Informant: Father	

Appendix: Buckingham County, Virginia Index of Death Records

Book/Page	Date	Decedent	Information	Identification
056	1884/12/02	Charles Wright	Place: Buckingham County, Virginia Race: Colored Sex: Male Age: 4 Parents Names: Charles & Susan Wright Birthplace: Buckingham Consort of: Single Informant: Charles Wright Relation of Informant: Father	1884 Charles Wright of Buckingham County, son of Charles Wright
059	1884/12/20	William Wright	Place: Buckingham County, Virginia Race: Colored Sex: Male Age: 25 Parents Names: C. L. & M. R. Wright Birthplace: Buckingham Occupation: Farmer Consort of: Married Informant: C. L. Wright Relation of Informant: Father	
051	1885/08/07	Wm. Iverson Wright	Place: Buckingham County, Virginia Race: Colored Sex: Male Age: 8 months Parents Names: Harry & Fannie Wright Birthplace: Buckingham Consort of: Unmarried Informant: Harry Wright Relation of Informant: Father	1885 William Iverson Wright of Buckingham County, son of Harry Wright and grandson of Billy Wright

Appendix: Buckingham County, Virginia Index of Death Records

Book/Page	Date	Decedent	Information	Identification
090	1887/01/00	Nannie Wright	Place: James River, Buckingham County, Virginia Race: Colored Sex: Female Age: 2 Cause: Pneumonia Parents Names: Willis & Louisa Wright Informant: Willis Wright Relation of Informant: Father	Nannie Wright, daughter of Willis Wright and granddaughter of 1892 Dick Wright of Buckingham County
012	1891/01/09	Margaret Wright	Place: Maysville District, Buckingham County, Virginia Race: White Sex: Female Age: 53 Cause: Cancer of Bones Consort of: W. D. Wright Informant: Charles H. Anderson Relation of Informant: Son	
020	1891/12/09	Louisa Wright	Place: Buckingham County, Virginia Race: Colored Sex: Female Age: 26 Cause: Milk Leg Birthplace: Maysville District Consort of: Willis Wright Informant: Willis Wright Relation of Informant: Husband	Lucy Ann or Louisa (Huddleston) Wright, wife of Willis Wright, a son of 1892 Dick Wright of Buckingham County

Book/Page	Date	Decedent	Information	Identification
001	1892/01/20	Dick Wright	Place: James River District, Buckingham County, Virginia Race: Colored Sex: Male Age: 86 Cause: Old Age Birthplace: James River District Occupation: Farmer Informant: Willis Wright Relation of Informant: Son	1892 Dick Wright of Buckingham County
001	1892/10/00	Eliza Wright	Place: James River District, Buckingham County, Virginia Race: Colored Sex: Female Age: 3 Cause: Flux Parents Names: Willis & _____ Wright Birthplace: Buckingham Consort of: Unmarried Informant: Willis Wright Relation of Informant: Father	Eliza Wright, daughter of Willis Wright and granddaughter of 1892 Dick Wright of Buckingham County
116	1892/12/20	Amanda Wright	Place: Buckingham County, Virginia Race: White Sex: Female Age: 40 Died December 20, 1892 Cause: Pneumonia Birthplace: Buckingham Occupation: Farmer Consort of: Single Informant: Lee Deane Relation of Informant: Friend	

Appendix: Buckingham County, Virginia Index of Death Records

Book/Page	Date	Decedent	Information	Identification
002	1893/09/09	Anna Wright	Place: James River District, Buckingham County, Virginia Race: Colored Sex: Female Age: 26 Cause: Consumption Birthplace: Buckingham Informant: Trent Wright Relation of Informant: Husband	Georgiana (Cabell) Wright, wife of Trent Wright, a son of 1892 Dick Wright of Buckingham County
011	1894/04/00	Maria Wright	Place: James River District, Buckingham County, Virginia Race: Colored Sex: Female Age: 13 Months Cause: Teething Parents Names: Bob & Alice Wright Relation of Informant: Father	
001	1894/05/00	Lillie Wright	Place: Maysville, Buckingham County, Virginia Race: White Sex: Female Age: 18 Months Cause: Cholera Infantum Parents Names: Wm. R. & Lillie Birthplace: Maysville Relation of Informant: Father	
087	1894/07/04	Betsy Wright	Place: Buckingham County, Virginia Race: Colored Sex: Female Age: 15 Cause: Scrofula Parents Names: Randolph & _____ Wright Informant: Randolph Wright Relation of Informant: Father	

Appendix: Buckingham County, Virginia Index of Death Records

Book/Page	Date	Decedent	Information	Identification
022	1895/04/06	Marie Elizabeth Wright	Place: Buckingham County, Virginia Race: Colored Sex: Female Age: 13 Months Cause: Teething Birthplace: Buckingham Consort of: Infant Informant: Bob Wright Relation of Informant: Father	
025	1895/10/04	Martha Wright	Place: Maysville District, Buckingham County, Virginia Race: Colored Sex: Female Age: 32 Cause: Childbirth Birthplace: Buckingham County Occupation: Wife Informant: Charity Moseley Relation of Informant: Friend	
016	1896/03/20	Mary L. Wright	Place: James River District, Buckingham County, Virginia Race: White Sex: Female Age: 27 Cause: Childbirth Birthplace: Buckingham Occupation: Farmer's Wife Informant: Jas. H. Davidson Relation of Informant: Friend	

Appendix: Buckingham County, Virginia Index of Death Records

Book/Page	Date	Decedent	Information	Identification
015	1896/05/15	Jas. E. Wright	Place: James River District, Buckingham County, Virginia Race: White Sex: Male Age: 2 Months Parents Names: _____ & Mary L. Wright Birthplace: Buckingham Occupation: Farmer's Son Consort of: Infant Informant: Jas. H. Davidson Relation of Informant: Friend	
	1913/06/15	Robert Wright	County: Buckingham County District: James River Sex: Male Color: Black Status: widowed Date of Birth: not Known Age: about 60 Occupation: Day laborer Birthplace: Virginia Father's name: Not Known Birthplace: Not Known Mother's name: Not Known Birthplace: Not Known Informant: J. H. Lewis Address: Toya Va Filed: August 11, 1913 Registrar: W. H. Spencer Cause: General dibility Length of Res: Buried: near Toya Date: June 17, 1913 Undertaker Willis Wright Address: Toya, Va	

Book/Page	Date	Decedent	Information	Identification
	1914/01/28	Maria Wright	County: Buckingham County District: Jas River Sex: Female Color: Mulatto Status: Widow Date of Birth: Age: 80 yrs Occupation: Servant, Farm hand Birthplace: Buckingham Va Father's name: unknown Birthplace: unknown Mother's name: Birthplace: Buckingham Va Informant: W. P. Ellis Address: Wily Va Filed: Feb 18th 1914 Registrar: W. H. Spencer Cause: Abdominal tumor Signed: G. L. Morris Address: Buckingham Length of Res: Buried: Buckingham Co Date: Jan 29th, 1914 Undertaker F. L. Ronson Address: Dillwyn Va	

Book/Page	Date	Decedent	Information	Identification
	1915/07/29	Ava _____ Wright	County: Buckingham County District: James River Sex: Female Color: Black Status: Single Date of Birth: May, 1915 Age: 2 mos Occupation: Birthplace: Virginia Father's name: Benjamin Wright Birthplace: Virginia Mother's name: Sallie Allen Birthplace: Buckingham Co. Va Informant: Ben Wright Address: Tower Hill, Va Filed: July 30, 1915 Registrar: F. W. Swan Cause: Spasms Length of Res: Buried: Date: July 30, 1915 Undertaker J. D. Ayers Address: Wingina	

Book/Page	Date	Decedent	Information	Identification
	1915/10/17	Thomas Wright	County: Buckingham County District: Curdsville Sex: Male Color: White Status: single Date of Birth: 1902 Age: 13 yrs Occupation: Birthplace: Buckingham Father's name: Jack Wright Birthplace: Buckingham Mother's name: Eva Tarry Birthplace: Cumberland Informant: M G Dunavant Address: Dilwyn Va Filed: October 18, 1915 Registrar: D. E. Hughes Cause: Fell out of tree & broke his back Length of Res: Buried: Cedar Church Date: October 18, 1915 Undertaker Fits Jerald & Ransom Address: Dillwyn Va	1915 William Thomas Wright of Buckingham County, son of 1925 Thomas Jackson Wright of Buckingham County, grandson of 1905 James A. Wright of Buckingham County, great grandson of 1863 William Wright of Buckingham County, great great grandson of 1803 John Wright of Cumberland County, great great great grandson of 1770 John Wright of Cumberland County, and great great great grandson of 1769 George Wright of Essex County

Book/Page	Date	Decedent	Information	Identification
	1917/06/30	____ Wright	County: Buckingham County	

County: Buckingham County
District: Jame River
Sex: Boy
Color: White
Status: Single
Date of Birth: June 30, 1917
Age: 8 hrs
Occupation: Infant
Birthplace: Va
Father's name: Thos. J. Wright
Birthplace: Buckingham Co Va
Mother's name: Georgia A. Wade
Birthplace: Buckingham Co Va
Filed: 7/10/17
Registrar: L. P. Gilliam
Cause: Premature birth born at 6 month
 of gestation
Signed: P. E. Tucker M.D.
Date: July 9 1917
Address: Buckingham
Length of Res:
Buried:
Date of Burial:
Undertaker:
Address:

Book/Page	Date	Decedent	Information	Identification
	1917/08/15	Trent Wright	County: Buckingham County District: James River Sex: Male Color: Colered Status: Married Date of Birth: Unknown Age: about 63 yrs Occupation: Shoemaker Birthplace: Buckingham Co Va Father's name: Richard Wright Birthplace: Buckingham Co Va Mother's name: Catherine Jones Birthplace: Buckingham Co Va Informant: George Bennett Address: Toya, Va Filed: 8/18/17 Registrar: T. P. Gilliam Cause: Asthma & Rheumatism, also old age Length of Res: Buried: Buckingham Co Va Date: Aug 16, 1917 Undertaker Gilmer & Bennett(?) Address: Toya Va	1912 Trent Wright of Buckingham County, son of 1892 Dick Wright of Buckingham County

Appendix: Buckingham County, Virginia Index of Death Records

Book/Page	Date	Decedent	Information	Identification
	1917/10/05	Maggie Wright	County: Buckingham County District: Curdsville Sex: Female Color: White Status: Married Date of Birth: October 8, 1893 Age: 24 yrs Occupation: None Birthplace: Buckingham Father's name: John D Jamerson Birthplace: Buckingham Mother's name: Mollie Childress Birthplace: Buckingham Informant: Joe Jamerson Address: Bolling, Va Filed: Oct 5, 1917 Registrar: E. W. Fitzgerald Cause: Carcinoma of Liver Duration: 2 yrs Signed: P. E. Tucker M.D. Date: Oct 29, 1917 Address: Buckingham, Va Length of Res: Buried: Family cemetery Date: Oct 6, 1917 Undertaker E W Fitzgerald Address: Dillwyn	

Book/Page	Date	Decedent	Information	Identification
	1918/12/15	William J Wright	County: Buckingham County District: James River Sex: Male Color: White Status: Single Date of Birth: March 18, 1886 Age: 32 yrs 7 mos 27 ds Occupation: Farmer Birthplace: Buckingham Co Father's name: William J Wright Birthplace: Buckingham Mother's name: Addie S McCaulder Birthplace: Buckingham Co Informant: A J Harriman Address: Tower Hill RF #1 Filed: 12/1/18 Registrar: L. P. Gilliam Cause: Influenza Broncho Pneumonia Signed: D. A. Christian M.D. Date: Dec 1918 Address: Heva, Fa Length of Res: Buried: Wright Buryal Ground Date: Dec 17, 1918 Undertaker E W Fitzgerald Address: Dillwyn Va	1918 William J. Wright of Buckingham County, son of William A. Jefferson Wright, grandson of 1873 Thomas F. Wright of Buckingham County, probably great grandson of 1842 Thomas Wright of Buckingham County, great great grandson of 1813 John Wright of Buckingham County, and great great great grandson of 1809 John Wright of Buckingham County

Book/Page	Date	Decedent	Information	Identification
	1919/01/09	Robert J Wright	County: Buckingham County District: James River Sex: Male Color: Col Status: Married Date of Birth: Age: 24 yrs Occupation: Laborer Birthplace: Buckingham Co Father's name: Robert Wright Birthplace: Buckingham Va Mother's name: Allice Clark Birthplace: Buckingham Informant: J A ____ Address: Wingina Filed: Mch 10 1919 Registrar: P. P. Glover Cause: Influenza Pneumonia Signed: G. L. Morris M.D. Date: Feb. 11th 1919 Address: Buckingham, Va Length of Res: Buried: Date of Burial: Undertaker: E W Fitzgerald Address: Dillwyn	1919 Robert J. Wright of Buckingham County, son of Robert Wright

Book/Page	Date	Decedent	Information	Identification
	1919/05/29	Bettie Lee Wright	County: Buckingham County District: James River Sex: female Color: white Status: Widow Date of Birth: Feb 11, 1841 Age: Occupation: Birthplace: Father's name: John L. Patterson Birthplace: Buckingham Mother's name: Janie Morris Birthplace: Albmarle Co. Virginia Informant: O. A. Wright Address: Wingina Va Filed: June 7, 1919 Registrar: F. W. Swan Cause: Infirmities of Old age Buried: Buckingham Co Date: May 3, 1919 Undertaker: W. A. Stinson Address: Wingina Va	Bettie Lee (Patterson) Wright, wife of Leonard H. Wright, a son of Charles Wright and grandson of Robert Wright, Sr., (Campbell County)

Appendix: Buckingham County, Virginia Index of Death Records

Book/Page	Date	Decedent	Information	Identification
	1920/04/15	Annie Wright	County: Buckingham County District: Curdsville Sex: Female Color: White Status: Married Born: S. S Wright Age: 36 years Occupation: none Birthplace: Buckingham Co Father's name: Pondexter Banton Birthplace: Virginia Mother's name: Manoah(?) Shoemaker Birthplace: Buckingham Co Informant: Edward Jamerson Address: Dillwyn Va Filed: April 15 1920 Registrar: E W Fitzgerald Cause: Influenza Signed: J. H. Mitchell M.D. Date: My 5 1920 Address: Dillwyn Va Buried: Rosney Va Date: Apr 2, 1920 Undertaker: Address:	Ann (Banton) Wright, wife of 1955 Seymour Smith Wright, a son of 1905 James A. Wright of Buckingham County, grandson of 1863 William Wright of Buckingham County, great grandson of 1803 John Wright of Cumberland County, great great grandson of 1770 John Wright of Cumberland County, and great great great grandson of 1769 George Wright of Essex County

Book/Page	Date	Decedent	Information	Identification
	1920/04/02	Houston Wright	County: Buckingham County District: Jas River Sex: Male Color: Black Status: Date of Birth: Sep, 1914 Age: 5 yrs Occupation: Birthplace: Buckingham Co Father's name: Robert Wright Birthplace: Buckingham Co Mother's name: Lizzie Booker Birthplace: Buckingham Co Informant: Archie Booker Address: W Tower Hill Va Filed: April 3 1920 Registrar: F W. Swan Cause: dropsy - no physician attended Length of Res: Buried: Buckingham Co Date: April 3rd, 1920 Undertaker: Paul Cabell Address: Brier Hook Va	1920 Houston Wright of Buckingham County, son of Robert Wright

Book/Page	Date	Decedent	Information	Identification
	1920/06/14	Thomas Uriah Wright	County: Buckingham County District: James River Sex: Male Color: White Status: Single Born: December 25, 1859 Age: 60 yrs 5 mos 14 ds Occupation: Farmer Birthplace: Buckingham Co. Va. Father's name: Thomas H. Wright Birthplace: Buckingham Co. Va. Mother's name: Susan W. Hardiman Birthplace: Charlotte Co. Virginia Informant: Clara A. Robterson Address: Brierhook, Va Filed: July 6, 1920 Registrar: F. W. Swan Cause: Not reported by informant, Angina Pectoris Length of Res: Buried: Buckingham Co. Date: June 16, 1920 Undertaker: J. W. Fitzgerald Address: Dillwyn, Va.	1920 Thomas Uriah Wright of Buckingham County, son of 1873 Thomas F. Wright of Buckingham County, probably grandson of 1842 Thomas Wright of Buckingham County, great grandson of 1813 John Wright of Buckingham County, and great great grandson of 1809 John Wright of Buckingham County

Book/Page	Date	Decedent	Information	Identification
	1920/12/10	Bertha Wright	County: Buckingham County District: James River nr Brierhook Va Sex: Female Color: Negro Status: married Born: June 10, 1891 Age: 29 yrs 6 mos Occupation: House work Birthplace: Lexington Va Father's Name: Birthplace: Mother's name: Ada Fyle Birthplace: Buckingham co Va Informant: Sam Wright Address: Brierhook Va Filed: 12/18/20 Registrar: L. P. Gilliam Cause: Unknown No doctor Length of Res: Buried: Buckingham Co Va nr Brierbrook Date: Decem 12, 1920 Undertaker: Thomas Clayborn Address: Brierhook Va.	

WRIGHT FAMILY

PROBATE RECORDS

1758 TO 1922

BUCKINGHAM COUNTY, VIRGINIA

Revised as of June 30, 2025

Introduction To Appendix: Probate Records for Buckingham County, Virginia

This document is an appendix to a larger work titled *Sorting Some Of The Wrights Of Southern Virginia*. The work is divided into parts for each family of Wrights that has been researched. Each part is divided into two sections; the first section is text discussing the family and the evidence supporting the relationships and the second section is a descendants chart summarizing the relationships and information known about each individual.

The appendices to the work (of which this document is one) present source records for persons named Wright by county and by type of record with the identification of the person named and their Wright ancestors to the extent known.

The sources for the records listed in this appendix are the following:

1) Buckingham County, Virginia, Probate Records, available from the Clerk of the Circuit Court, P.O. Box 107, Buckingham, Virginia 23921.

2) Genealogical Records of Buckingham County, Virginia, by Edythe Rucker Whitely, Genealogical Publishing Co., Inc., 1984.

The identification of a person or their ancestor by year and county indicates their year of death and county of residence at death. For example, "1763 Thomas Wright of Bedford County" indicates that this was the Thomas Wright who died in 1763 in Bedford County. If no state is listed after the county, the state is Virginia; counties in states other than Virginia will have a state listed after the county, as in "1876 William S. Wright of Highland County, Ohio".

A parenthetical after the name indicates an identification of the person when a place of death is not yet known, as in "John Wright (Goochland County Carpenter)". A county in parentheses after the name indicates the county with which that person was most identified when no evidence of the place of death has yet been found, as in "Grief Wright (Bedford County)".

All or portions of the text and descendants charts for each Wright family identified are available from the author:

Robert N. Grant
15 Campo Bello Court   (H) 415-854-0895
Menlo Park, California 94025   RNGrant@grantandgordon.com

This is a work in progress and I would be most interested in receiving additional information about any of the persons identified in these records in order to correct any errors or expand on the information given.

0182(063025)

Appendix: Buckingham County, Virginia, Probate Records:

Book/Page		Date	Decedent	Instrument	Identification
1	401	1891/11/09	James A. Wright	Will	1891 James A. Wright of Buckingham County, son of 1842 Thomas Wright of Buckingham County, grandson of 1813 John Wright of Buckingham County, and great grandson of 1809 John Wright of Buckingham County
1	402	1891/11/12	Frances Wright	Renunciation of provision of will of husband	Frances Ann (____) Wright, widow of 1891 James A. Wright of Buckingham County, a son of 1842 Thomas Wright of Buckingham County, grandson of 1813 John Wright of Buckingham County, and great grandson of 1809 John Wright of Buckingham County
1	403	1892/01/11	Frances A. Wright	Will	Frances Ann (____) Wright, widow of 1891 James A. Wright of Buckingham County, a son of 1842 Thomas Wright of Buckingham County, grandson of 1813 John Wright of Buckingham County, and great grandson of 1809 John Wright of Buckingham County
2	331	1922/04/22	T. U. Wright,	Account Admin. Acct.	1920 Thomas Uriah Wright of Buckingham County, son of 1873 Thomas F. Wright of Buckingham County, probably grandson of 1842 Thomas Wright of Buckingham County, great grandson of 1813 John Wright of Buckingham County, and great great grandson of 1809 John Wright of Buckingham County

Heritage Books by Robert N. Grant

Lynchburg

Wright Family Records: Lynchburg, Virginia Birth Records (1853–1896), Marriage Records (1805–1900), Marriage Notices (1794–1880), Census Records (1900), Deed Records (1805–1900), Death Records (1853–1896), Probate Records (1805–1900)

Amherst County

Wright Family Birth Records, 1853–1896; Marriage Records, 1761–1900; Census Records, 1810–1900, in Amherst County, Virginia

Wright Family Land Tax Records: Amherst County, Virginia, 1782–1850

Wright Family Patent Deeds and Land Grants, 1761–1900, Deed Records, 1761–1903; Chancery Court Files, 1804–1900; Death Records, 1853–1920; Cemetery Records by Cemetery; and Probate Records, 1761–1900, in Amherst County, Virginia

Wright Family Personal Property Tax Lists: Amherst County, Virginia, 1782–1850

Appomattox County

Wright Family Birth Records, Marriage Records, and Personal Property Tax Lists: Appomattox County, Virginia

Wright Family Census Records, Deed Records, Land Tax Lists, Death Records and Probate Records: Appomattox County, Virginia

Bedford County

Wright Family Census Records: Bedford County, Virginia, 1810–1900

Wright Family Death, Cemetery and Probate Records: Bedford County, Virginia

Wright Family Land Records: Bedford County, Virginia

Wright Family Personal Property Tax Records for Bedford County, Virginia, 1782 to 1850

Wright Family Records: Births in Bedford County, Virginia

Wright Family Records: Land Tax List, Bedford County, Virginia, 1782–1850

Wright Family Records: Marriages in Bedford County, Virginia

Botetourt County

Wright Family Birth, Marriage, and Personal Property Tax Records: Botetourt County, Virginia

Wright Family Census, Deed, Land Tax, Death and Probate Records: Botetourt County, Virginia

Buckingham County

Wright Family Records. Buckingham County, Virginia. Birth Records, 1853–1896; Marriage Records, 1758–1933; Personal Property Tax Lists, 1782–1860; Census Records, 1810–1900

Wright Family Records. Buckingham County, Virginia Patent Deeds and Land Grants; Deed Records, 1758–1908; Land Tax Lists, 1782–1850; Death Records, 1856–1920; Probate Records, 1758–1922

Campbell County

Wright Family Birth Records (1853–1896) and Marriage Records (1782–1900): Campbell County, Virginia

Wright Family Census Records: Campbell County, Virginia, 1810–1900

Wright Family Death Records (1853–1920), Cemetery Records by Cemetery, and Probate Records (1782–1900): Campbell County, Virginia

Wright Family Deed Records (1782–1900) and Land Tax List (1782–1850): Campbell County, Virginia

Wright Family Personal Property Tax Lists: Campbell County, Virginia, 1785–1850

Rockbridge County

Wright Family Birth Records, 1853–1896; Marriage Records, 1777–1918; Census Records, 1810–1900; Deed Records, 1777–1902; Death Records, 1853–1896; Cemetery Records, and Probate Records, 1777–1909; in Rockbridge County, Virginia

Wright Family Land Tax Lists: Rockbridge County, Virginia, 1782–1850

Wright Family Personal Property Tax Lists: Rockbridge County, Virginia, 1782–1850

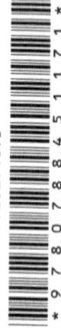